# RECIPES
# FROM A
# POLISH
# KITCHEN

# RECIPES FROM A POLISH KITCHEN

## BRIDGET JONES

*Very special thanks are due to Małgosia Curtis and Eva Biestega for their notes, recipe ideas, advice, and for sampling and commenting on the cooking.*

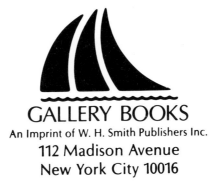

## GALLERY BOOKS
An Imprint of W. H. Smith Publishers Inc.
112 Madison Avenue
New York City 10016

**A QUINTET BOOK**

produced for
GALLERY BOOKS
An imprint of W.H. Smith Publishers Inc.
112 Madison Avenue
New York, New York 10016

ISBN 0-8317-7061-9

This book was designed and produced by
Quintet Publishing Limited
6 Blundell Street
London N7 9BH

Creative Director: Peter Bridgewater
Art Director: Ian Hunt
Project Editor: Caroline Beattie
Editor: Barbara Croxford
Photographer: Derek St Romaine
Home Economist: Joyce Harrison
Stylist: Dawn St Romaine

Typeset in Great Britain by
Central Southern Typesetters, Eastbourne
Manufactured in Hong Kong by
Regent Publishing Services Limited
Printed in Hong Kong by
Leefung-Asco Printers Limited

The Publishers would also like to thank
Polorbis Travel Ltd for supplying the pictures on
pages 23, 37, and 92 and
Tim Sharman of the European Geographic
Survey for supplying the pictures on
pages 7, 8, 46 and 77.

## DEDICATION

*To Neill, for tasting all the dishes, commenting and
encouraging even after helping to clear the kitchen.*

# CONTENTS

# INTRODUCTION

Even a cursory glance through a book on Polish history reveals centuries of strife, unrest and uncertainty. Generations of mixed sovereignty and frequently changing frontiers are the result of battles and wars that seem to have dominated the country and its people for centuries. Yet throughout this chequered history the Poles have retained a firm identity of their own, a distinct culture and a cherished cuisine.

A trio of influences has probably played a key role in the survival of traditional Polish cooking. The geographical and climatic characteristics of the country play their part. Situated with a narrow stretch at the most northern end coasting the Baltic sea, Poland is surrounded by Russia, Czechoslovakia and Germany. The majority of the country does not have access to the sea and its primary source of food is through agriculture, with hardy root vegetables and cabbages surviving the harsh climate. Poland is known for its game, venison and wild boar in particular, and for fresh water fish, notably carp. In a country where the cold is cruel, wholesome, no-nonsense cooking is essential, with soups and stews to provide winter warmth and filling foods to keep away the cold of hunger.

The third influence, that of religion, is no less strong; indeed its doctrines may be credited for establishing many culinary customs. Poland has a long history of Catholicism which sets it apart from neighbouring Russia and Germany. Education and travel came to Poland through the early church and the religious calendar provided fasts and feasts which grew to dominate the ancient pagan rites.

GROUPS OF PEOPLE RETURNING FROM CHURCH IN DZIANISZ.

## A TRAVELLED GENTRY

The great families of Poland were well travelled and sociable. They visited other European countries and allowed foreigners to live in their own nation, at the same time taking on some of the social style introduced by the outsiders. This, combined with the neighbours who fought, won, lost and battled time and time again over the rulership of Poland, created a cuisine that provides far more than the essentials demanded by the climate.

Traditionally, Poland is a nation of great meat eaters, a characteristic that survived through many hundreds of years. A sixteenth century queen of Poland, Bona Sforza, who came from Milan to marry King Sigismund I, was horrified at the quantities of meat and lack of vegetables that were consumed. So she began the process of introducing variety to the diet in the way of fresh vegetables and other foods such as pasta. Many of the dumplings, the use of garlic and even the famous Easter Babka owe a certain amount to the Italian influence.

The Jewish population of Poland also contributed their ideas to the cooking and these are particularly noticeable in the preparation of cold platters of fish in aspic, for example.

THE POTATO HARVEST IN BUKOWINA, IN THE TATRA MOUNTAINS.

## COFFEE AND CAKE

By way of contrast to the savouries and meals, Poland is renowned for its coffee houses where wonderful gâteaux and pastries, similar to those of Austria, are served. Taking coffee and cake in Polish cafés is very much a social event, an occasion to share with friends or an opportunity for entertaining. As well as the spectacular creations reserved for special occasions, simpler cakes and pastries are eaten as everyday refreshments.

## FASTS AND FEASTS

Two main religious feasts dominate the year and the most important of these is Christmas. Christmas eve is both a time for fasting, when meat is not eaten, and a time for celebrating. The celebration meal is served in the evening, and only when the first star is visible in the sky. Children anxiously peer out of the windows awaiting the first sign of a glisten in the sky, for when the meal is over there are presents to be unwrapped.

Traditionally the Christmas eve meal consists of 12 courses, one for each of the apostles. Clear beetroot (beet) soup, barszcz, is served with tiny dumplings, uszka or little ears. In some households, a soup of dried mushrooms may be served. The centrepiece of the meal is carp, traditionally served coated in a sweet-sour sauce with raisins and almonds. It is eaten either cold or hot. Alternatively, the carp may be served hot with a horseradish sauce.

A selection of vegetable accompaniments and sweet dishes are offered. One of the oldest of sweet dishes is a bowl of noodles tossed with honey and poppy seeds. A sweet yeast dough and poppy seed roll, at least two highly decorated gâteaux, some delicate biscuits (cookies) with a poppy seed dip and a large bowl of dried fruit compote are all prepared for the Christmas eve celebration. Beautifully decorated biscuits, some very large and cut in the shape of hearts, are tied on the Christmas tree.

A small amount of straw is placed under the tablecloth to represent the manger in which Jesus was born and ears of wheat are placed in the corners of the room to bring good fortune in the year that is to follow.

Needless to say, there is usually enough in the way of sweet dishes to provide for Christmas day, when goose or turkey are served for the main meal.

## NEW YEAR CELEBRATIONS

New Year's Eve is another opportunity for feasting, when the meal may consist of a special joint of cold roast veal with buffet-style food or perhaps a steaming pot of bigos – an ancient hunter's stew. The period from New Year through to the beginning of Lent is a time for celebrating and socializing. In Poland, Sunday afternoon is a popular time for inviting friends and family for coffee (or tea) and a selection of home baked gâteaux or other cakes.

## EASTER

Although Easter is not the main event on the religious calendar, it is the second most important feast of the year. On Easter Sunday, everyone gathers for breakfast after paying their morning visit to church.

The Easter breakfast breaks the lenten fast in a feast that extends throughout the day, with lamb (a meat otherwise rarely eaten) as the main course. A babka, a rich yeasted cake, baked in a tall, fluted kugelhopf mould and decorated with a sugar paste lamb, tiny Easter eggs and sprigs of fresh green foliage, is the speciality for Easter. Cheesecake and mazurek, a rich type of shortbread, are also prepared.

## SAINTS' DAYS

Birthdays are quiet occasions but in their place the saint's day after whom each person takes their name is the excuse for a celebration. A gâteau, tall with many layers and richly decorated with piped cream, is served to friends and gifts are given to the person who is celebrating.

## MODERN COOKING RICH IN CUSTOM

The fact that so many old recipes and customs have survived makes Polish cooking rather special. Splendid use is made of simple ingredients, stretching inexpensive foods to make tempting meals. Fresh produce in season and preserved foods are combined to complement each other. Ingenuity is evident in the ways in which vegetables are turned into the main part of so many meals. The uncomplicated approach is refreshing compared to the intricacies of the cooking of other nations.

Soured cream, salted herrings and fresh horseradish are used in many recipes. Wild mushrooms grow in abundance in Poland. They are gathered and dried, hung by stringing them on thread, then used to flavour a wide variety of dishes. Summer fruits are preserved by bottling them in spirit or in syrup, or the fruit may be made into syrups for flavouring desserts.

Beer is served rather than wine with a Polish meal, or mead may be offered on special occasions. Vodka and a wide variety of flavoured spirits, some infused with herbs others fragrant with fruit, are drunk either before or after a meal. Before an important meal, or in honour of a special event, the custom is to drink Polish vodka thoroughly chilled with a variety of canapés and pickles.

In the chapters that follow you will find a selection of the better known Polish recipes as well as many everyday dishes. As far as possible I have tried to include notes, serving suggestions and comments on the flavours and seasonings. I hope you enjoy cooking and sampling the recipes as much as I have enjoyed discovering, testing and tasting them.

# GLOSSARY

**Bain-marie** A pan or roasting tin of hot water in which containers of delicate food are stood while they cook. The bain marie may be placed in the oven or used on the hob. Its purpose is to moderate the amount of heat that reaches the outside of the container of food, to prevent curdling or shrinkage.

**Bottled fruit** Look out for Polish bottled fruit in good delicatessens. Whole plums, cherries and other fruit are bottled in syrup or in Polish spirit. They are an excellent dessert ingredient.

**Buckwheat** Available from healthfood shops, buckwheat is usually sold roasted. The grains are small and slightly angular in shape. Although it is thought of as a cereal, buckwheat is not a true cereal in botanical terms. It is cooked in about 1½–2 times its volume of water by bringing it to the boil, then leaving the grain to absorb the liquid. Butter is forked into the buckwheat which is then known as kasha. Kasha is a popular accompaniment for meats and stews; it is also used to stuff cabbage leaves.

**Buckwheat flour** This fine, slightly brown-grey flour is available from healthfood stores. This may be used to make a gruel or it may be used in place of wheat flour in certain recipes. It gives the cooked dish a distinct, nutty flavour.

**Carp** This is a fresh water fish of which there are many different species, including goldfish. Carp has a reputation for having a 'muddy' flavour and the larger fish are very coarse. However, if you order carp from the fishmonger you will buy a farmed fish. The fish must not be too small or large and it must be perfectly fresh. Ask the fishmonger to scale the fish as the scales are large and they do get everywhere, even if you are careful about holding the fish down in the sink under running water. The cooking smell is not altogether pleasant but the poached flesh is moist, white and it has a delicate flavour. It cannot be compared directly with white sea fish such as cod or haddock, which are drier, more distinctive in flavour and with flesh that flakes; it is better to compare it with a large salmon trout for texture. Carp has lots of very large, fine bones.

**Celery root** Eastern European recipes often call for celery root. Celeriac is a root vegetable with a flavour similar to celery. Although it does, apparently, differ from Polish celery root it is an acceptable substitute which I have used throughout the recipes.

**Chives** Slim, grass-like strands of a herb with an onion-like flavour, chives are very popular in Polish cooking. They are added to savoury butters and spreads or sprinkled over salads and soups. Hold the whole bunch of chives and wash them under cold running water, then dry on absorbent kitchen paper. Chives are not usually chopped: use a pair of kitchen scissors to snip them into small pieces ready for use. They are referred to as 'snipped chives'.

**Cottage cheese** Polish cottage cheese has a bland flavour similar to the soft curds which are obtainable in cartons. However, it has a firm texture and may be cut with a knife. The difference in texture causes a problem when preparing recipes such as baked cheesecake. However, this can be overcome to a certain extent either by draining the cottage cheese through muslin (cheesecloth) by hanging it overnight or by squeezing out excess liquid.

**Dill** Dill is a very popular herb in Polish cooking. It is used with fish, vegetables, in sauces or stuffings and with poultry. Fresh dill has a delicate and refreshing flavour which is far superior to dried dill (sometimes referred to as 'dill weed'). Dill looks very similar to fennel, a herb which has an aniseed flavour, but its feathery leaves are slightly shorter and more bushy than fennel. The real distinction is in flavour. Fennel may not be substituted for dill. Dill is available from good supermarkets. It may be chopped and frozen.

**Fat** Certain recipes call for 'fat' rather than specifying the use of oil or butter for cooking. Ideally, the fat used should be meat dripping which imparts a flavour to the food in which it is cooked. Oil or butter can be used instead.

**Fermented beetroot (beet) juice** Bottles of this juice are available from continental delicatessens or from some healthfood stores. The juice is not sour but, unlike fresh beetroot, it is slightly piquant. It is added to beetroot soup to counteract the natural sweetness of the vegetable. Just a little lemon juice or cider vinegar may usually be substituted, however both are more harsh in flavour.

**Horseradish** An essential ingredient for a variety of Polish recipes. Hot horseradish sauce is served with boiled meat or with fish. Grated fresh horseradish is also added to salads or served with herrings. Horseradish grows very easily but it must be dug and replanted to produce roots that are thick enough to peel and grate easily. The leaves of the plant are large and they look a little like dock leaves. The root must be scrubbed and peeled, then grated or finely processed in a food processor or blender. Fresh horseradish is far better than bought varieties. It may be preserved in white vinegar (good sweetened) or it freezes well. In place of the fresh root, use dried grated horseradish, soaked in the minimum of water until soft, or horseradish sauce. Creamed horseradish has a milder flavour. A word of warning – do not rub your eyes when peeling fresh horseradish as it stings, and be prepared to shed a few tears over the task!

**Juniper berries** These small round, dried berries are about the same size as black peppercorns. These have a strong flavour so they are usually used sparingly. They are the ingredient which gives gin its distinctive flavour. Juniper berries are used to flavour venison and other game.

**Kabanos** This long, thin smoked Polish cooked sausage is readily available from supermarkets and delicatessens. Delicious with sauerkraut or cabbage.

**Mushrooms, dried** Wild mushrooms grow in abundance in Poland where they are picked and dried. They are threaded on strings to hang in a clean dry place and may be purchased off the strings from Polish delicatessens. Other varieties of dried mushroom are available from most good delicatessens, either whole or sliced (usually cheaper and not as good quality). Dried mushrooms are expensive but they do go a long way. One or two will flavour a sauce or stew well, more are used for making soup or stuffing.

The dried mushrooms should be simmered in water – just to cover them in a small pan – for about 5 minutes, or until they are tender enough to cut up. The liquid should never be discarded: if it is not required for the particular recipe, strain, cool and freeze it for flavouring soups, sauces and stews.

**Pickled mushrooms** These mushrooms are available from delicatessens, particularly Polish ones. These may be pickled in brine or in a vinegar mixture; they may be bottled on their own or with other vegetables. Pickled mushrooms are served with vodka or used as a topping for canapés.

**Plum spread** This is a preserve made of sweet plums. It is similar to a fruit butter in texture and usually available in jars from Polish delicatessens. Check the label for added sugar which should be minimum. The spread is quite tangy and it may be used as a filling for doughnuts or for sandwiching cakes in layers.

**Polish spirit** Polish spirit varies in strength but it is always very strong. Wine stores do stock spirit as well as vodka. The spirit may be used to preserve fruit (with a certain amount of syrup) or it may be used in some drinks (krupnik, see page 22).

**Poppy seeds** Some baked goods call for large quantities of poppy seeds. Buy poppy seeds that are to be used in this way from good delicatessens (preferably Polish) where they are sold in large packets and where the turnover is such that they will be fresh. The poppy seeds should be blue-grey in colour.

The traditional method of grinding the poppy seeds is to pour freshly boiling water over them and leave to cool. They are then drained, squeezed out in muslin (cheesecloth) and put through a hand mincer (grinder). The seeds are minced twice through the finest blade. The result is a fine paste, no whole seeds and no gritty texture.

I have tried using a blender and food processor – do not bother as it is a waste of time, neither give results that are good enough. However, the most efficient method is to grind the unsoaked, dry, seeds in a coffee grinder. Make sure that the grinder is absolutely clean, wiping it out with damp absorbent kitchen paper, then drying it. Grind small quantities of the dry seeds at a time. Do not overload the coffee grinder. It is quick and easy to do.

**Rye flour** Available from healthfood stores, this flour is used for making rye bread. It is usually used in equal proportions with wheat flour. The dough is heavy to work compared to dough made with wheat flour alone.

**Salted herrings** These are available packed in oil from the chiller cabinet of good delicatessens. Always check the sell-by date, although they do have a long shelf life. Mop the herrings on absorbent kitchen paper to remove all the oil of packing before using. Alternatively, rollmops packed in brine may be used. Rollmops in a sweet-sour vinegar preserve do not have the same flavour as salted herrings.

**Sauerkraut** Available in jars from supermarkets and delicatessens, sauerkraut is packed in tangy brine. It should be drained and squeezed out. When it is squeezed it stays in a firm pat which is easy to slice across into pieces. The juice may be added to some dishes to make them more sour.

Sauerkraut is prepared by salting shredded fresh cabbage. The cabbage and salt are layered in an earthenware container to form a brine. The brine must be kept topped up so that the cabbage is completely covered. The cabbage ferments which gives it the sour flavour. After a certain number of days the fermented cabbage is packed in brine for storage. Sauerkraut should only be prepared following a reputable recipe to avoid any danger of bacterial spoilage of the cabbage, which may cause food poisoning.

**Soured cream** This has a number of uses, for example in soups, sauces, stews, pastry doughs, salads and vegetable dishes. Cream is soured by the addition of a culture which is allowed to ferment briefly. The resulting cream has a fresh tang rather than a very sour flavour. It is readily available from larger supermarkets.

**Speck** This is solid smoked bacon fat with a coating of paprika. It is German and not readily available, although some good delicatessens do stock it. Alternatively, cured fat is to be found in Polish delicatessens. Diced fat is rendered and browned, then used as a topping for a number of savoury dishes, particularly dumplings.

**Weijska** These large smoked sausage rings are available from good delicatessen counters in large supermarkets or small delicatessens. It is a chunky ham and pork sausage which is well flavoured with garlic. Delicious in bigos or served boiled and sliced with cabbage or sauerkraut.

**Yeast** Fresh yeast (compressed yeast) is usually available from any shop which bakes bread on the premises. Try small bakers or the hot bread shops in supermarkets. Sometimes they may sell a fast-action yeast which causes the dough to rise faster than ordinary fresh yeast.

Fresh yeast should have a pleasant smell, it should be cool, crumbly and grey-beige in colour. It will keep in the refrigerator, in a plastic bag, for two to three days or it may be frozen for up to three months.

Dried yeast may be used instead of fresh yeast. There are two types of dried yeast so check the instructions on the packet. Ordinary dried yeast is sprinkled over liquid and left to become frothy before being incorporated with the other ingredients. Easy blend dried yeast must be mixed with the dry ingredients before the liquid is added.

**Yeast doughs** Many sweet yeast doughs take a while to rise to double their size. Always put the dough in a covered bowl to prevent the surface from drying out. Put the bowl in a warm place, near a radiator or in a warm grill (broiler) compartment. Do not overheat the dough. Never be impatient with the dough – if it is not allowed to rise sufficiently the baking will be unsuccessful.

**Weighting pâté** Cooked pâtés are weighted to give them a firm texture. Cover the top of the pâté with foil or paper and put scale weights on top. If the pâté is in a round container, a small plate should be put under the weights. A clean building brick, wrapped in a couple of thicknesses of foil, is useful for weighting pâté. Stand the weighted pâté on a baking tin or in a dish to catch any juices that seep out. Leave overnight in the refrigerator.

# 1

# APPETIZERS

Everyday meals are unlikely to be preceded by a first course but for a special occasion it is traditional to serve a spread of canapés with small dishes of pickles before the meal. Well-chilled Polish vodka is served to wash down the savouries and to warm the gathered company through and through!

Soup is a popular first course along with salted herrings served in a variety of ways. Various creamy spreads or stuffed eggs may be served. Peeled, halved boiled eggs are usually stuffed but there is another clever method of stuffing the eggs in their shells – although these are more a snack than a starter you will find them in this chapter.

Small yeasted savouries, shaped into rolls and filled with flavoursome stuffings, may be served with vodka or as part of a buffet spread. Whatever the choice of recipe, the appetizer is always beautifully garnished and the canapés should form a dazzling display of culinary artistry.

## COTTAGE CHEESE SPREAD

Although Polish cottage cheese has a bland flavour similar to the cottage cheese we buy in cartons, it is white and firm enough to cut into crumbly slices. Serve this simple spread with rye bread or use it as a topping for canapés (page 19). Serves 4.

| |
|---|
| 1½ cups / 350 g / 12 oz cottage cheese |
| 4 tbsp soured cream |
| 1 pickled cucumber (dill pickle), diced |
| 1 tbsp chopped fresh dill |
| salt and freshly ground black pepper |
| dill sprigs to garnish (optional) |

Turn the cottage cheese out on to a double thick piece of scalded muslin (cheesecloth). Gather up the ends of the cloth and twist them together to squeeze as much liquid as possible from it.

Put the cheese in a bowl, using a spatula to scrape all the dry curds off the muslin, and mash it with a fork. Stir in the soured cream, pickled cucumber (dill pickle) and dill, adding seasoning to taste. Spoon the mixture into a serving dish and chill for about 30 minutes. Garnish with dill, if liked, before serving.

## EWE'S CHEESE WITH PAPRIKA

This spread is good with rye bread or it may be used on canapés (page 19). Try healthfood stores for ewe's cheese or use a good feta cheese instead. Serves 4.

| |
|---|
| ¼ lb / 100 g / 4 oz ewe's cheese |
| 6 tbsp soured cream |
| ½ tsp paprika |
| 1 tbsp snipped chives |

Mash the cheese with a fork, then gradually work in the soured cream to make a smooth paste. Stir in the paprika and chives. Chill lightly before serving with rye bread.

HERRING AND APPLE SALAD

## HERRING AND APPLE SALAD

Salted herrings and rollmops are widely used in southern Poland where fresh fish rarely makes an appearance in shops or on menus. This salad may be served as an appetizer or as a light main dish. I have cut the herrings into small strips but traditionally they would be served in large pieces, laid on the other salad ingredients. Serves 4.

| |
|---|
| 3 salted herring fillets |
| ¼ cucumber, peeled and thinly sliced (about ¼ lb / 100 g / 4 oz) |
| ½ onion, thinly sliced |
| 1 pickled cucumber (dill pickle), thinly sliced |
| 2 crisp, green eating apples, cored, quartered and thinly sliced |
| 1 tsp cider vinegar |
| 1 tbsp chopped fresh dill |
| 4 tbsp soured cream |

Remove any bones from the herring fillets, then cut them into small strips. Mix the herring, cucumber, onion, pickled cucumber (dill pickle) and apple with the vinegar.

Spoon the mixture on to a plate and sprinkle with dill. Trickle the soured cream over the salad and serve at once.

## HERRING SPREAD

This simple spread tastes delicious with fresh rye bread. It may also be served as an accompaniment to steak or on canapés (page 19). Serves 4.

*1 salted herring fillet (about 50 g/2 oz)*

*6 tbsp/75 g/3 oz unsalted butter*

*2 parsley sprigs*

*2 dill sprigs*

Mash the herring fillet, removing any remaining bones, or purée it in a food processor. Cream the butter to soften it, then work in the mashed herring. Chop the herbs and mix them into the spread. Serve with rye bread or use on canapés.

## HERRINGS IN SOURED CREAM

A simple appetizer that is particularly popular with or without the addition of hard-boiled egg (hard-cooked egg). Serve fresh rye bread as an accompaniment. Serves 4.

*4 salted herring fillets*

*1¼ cups/300 ml/½ pt soured cream*

*2 tbsp chopped fresh parsley or dill*

*½ small onion, finely chopped*

*2 eggs, hard-boiled (hard-cooked) and chopped*

*parsley or dill sprigs to garnish (optional)*

Mop the herring fillets on absorbent kitchen paper, then place them on individual plates.

Spoon the soured cream on to the plates, partly covering one end of each of the fillets. Sprinkle a little chopped parsley or dill over the soured cream. Arrange small piles of chopped onion and egg on each plate. Garnish with the herb sprigs, if used.

## FISH IN ASPIC

In Poland the fish would probably be carp but I have used cod fillet and a good fish stock for the maximum flavour. Fish in aspic is a popular alternative to carp for the Christmas eve meal. For the celebration meal, the whole carp would be poached and coated in aspic rather than serving portions of fish. Serves 4.

*½ lb/225 g/8 oz small cod fillets*

*1¼ cups/300 ml/½ pt fish stock (see below)*

*salt and freshly ground black pepper*

*8 thin carrot slices*

*4 thin leek slices*

*4 small dill sprigs*

*1 egg white and egg shell*

*1 tsp gelatine*

To skin the fillet, lay it skin side down on a board. Salt your fingertips and hold the tail of the fillet firmly. Use a sharp knife and hold it at an acute angle, then cut between the flesh and the skin of the fish. Use a sawing action, working from side to side of the fillet and fold back the skinned flesh as you cut. Use the skin, fish heads and other trimmings to make a good stock (see below).

Cut the fish into four portions and place them in a pan. Pour in the fish stock and add seasoning. Heat gently until simmering, then continue to cook for 3–5 minutes, until the fish is firm. Baste the fish during cooking if it is not completely covered with stock. Lift the pieces of fish from the stock, draining them well. Cool, covered, on a serving plate, then chill.

Simmer the vegetable slices in the stock for 1–2 minutes, until bright but still crisp. Drain. Arrange the vegetable slices on the fish.

Strain the stock into a small, perfectly clean saucepan. Scald a metal sieve and a piece of muslin (cheesecloth) in boiling water. Add the egg white and crushed egg shell to the stock. Heat gently, whisking all the time, until a thick froth forms on the surface. Stop whisking and allow the stock to boil up. Remove the pan from the heat, cool slightly, then put it back so that the stock boils up again. Repeat once more. If you have a gas hob, lower the heat rather than lifting the pan off the hob.

Strain the stock through the muslin-lined sieve into a perfectly clean, heatproof bowl. The stock should be sparkling clear. Sprinkle the gelatine into the stock and stir until it has dissolved completely. If necessary, place the bowl over a saucepan of simmering water to dissolve the gelatine. Leave to cool, then chill until beginning to set – the aspic should be syrup-like when poured off a spoon.

Coat the fish and vegetables with aspic, then chill until completely set. Use a pointed knife to trim the aspic from the edges of the fish before serving.

**FISH STOCK** Use fish heads, bones, skin and other trimmings for stock. The fishmonger will supply these if you are not using whole fish. Place the trimmings in a pan with a bay leaf, parsley sprig, 4 black peppercorns, 1 roughly chopped onion and 1 sliced carrot. Pour in cold water to cover and bring to the boil. Reduce the heat, cover and simmer for 1 hour. Cool, then strain through muslin (cheesecloth). Bones cause the stock to gel when chilled.

## FISH SALAD

A delicate salad that may be served as a light main course as well as for the first course of the meal. Serves 4.

| |
|---|
| ½ lb / 225 g / 8 oz cod fillet |
| 1¼ cups / 300 ml / ½ pt fish stock (see above) |
| 1 medium potato, cooked and cooled |
| 1 pickled cucumber (dill pickle), sliced |
| ¼ cucumber, peeled and diced (about ¼ lb / 100 g / 4 oz) |
| 2 tbsp snipped chives |
| ⅔ cup / 150 ml / ¼ pt soured cream |
| 1 tbsp horseradish sauce |
| salt and freshly ground black pepper |
| 24 cucumber slices to garnish |

Place the fish in a shallow pan. Pour in the stock and heat until simmering. Poach gently for 3–5 minutes, until the fish is firm and just cooked. Set the fish aside to cool in the stock.

Dice the potato and mix it with the pickled and fresh cucumber. Drain the fish and flake the flesh off the skin, removing all bones. Stir the chives, soured cream and horseradish into the vegetables, adding seasoning to taste. Add the fish and mix very lightly to avoid breaking the flakes. Divide the salad between four small plates and garnish with cucumber.

CARAWAY BREADSTICKS

## CARAWAY BREADSTICKS

Serve these with Polish vodka or as an accompaniment to soup. Makes about 50.

| |
|---|
| 1 tsp (active) dried yeast or 15 g / ½ oz fresh yeast (½ cake compressed yeast) |
| 2 tbsp lukewarm water |
| 1 tsp sugar |
| 2 cups / 225 g / 8 oz strong white flour (hard wheat flour) |
| 1 tsp salt |
| 2 tbsp / 25 g / 1 oz butter |
| 2 tsp caraway seeds |
| 4 tbsp soured cream |

Sprinkle the dried yeast over the water and sugar. Cream the fresh yeast with the water and sugar. Leave in a warm place until frothy.

Sift the flour and salt into a bowl, then rub in the butter. Add the caraway seeds and make a well in the middle. Pour in the yeast liquid, stir in the soured cream, then mix in the dry ingredients to make a stiff dough. Knead thoroughly for 10 minutes, until smooth and elastic. Place the dough in a bowl, cover with cling film (plastic wrap); and leave in a warm place until doubled in size – at least 1 hour. Grease two baking sheets. Set the oven at 220°C / 425°F / gas 7.

Lightly knead the dough and cut it into quarters. Roll each piece into a long, thin roll (about pencil thickness) and cut into 5–7.5 cm / 2–3 in lengths. Place the sticks on the baking sheets. Bake for 12–15 minutes, until golden and crisp. Cool on a wire rack.

STUFFED EGGS

## STUFFED EGGS

These are a little difficult to make but they are quite unusual and delicious – well worth the effort involved in avoiding breaking the egg shell into the stuffing. Serves 4.

*5 eggs*

*1 small onion, finely chopped*

*2 tbsp / 25 g / 1 oz butter*

*½ tsp dried marjoram*

*2 tbsp soured cream*

*salt and freshly ground black pepper*

*1 cup / 75 g / 3 oz dry white breadcrumbs*

*2 tbsp oil*

*1 lettuce heart, shredded*

*1 tomato, sliced, to garnish*

Boil four of the eggs for 10 minutes. Drain and put under running cold water to cool. Take good care not to crack the shells.

Cook the onion in the butter over a gentle heat for 10 minutes, until very soft but not browned. Add the marjoram and set aside. Use a sharp serrated knife to carefully 'saw' the unshelled eggs in half lengthways. Trim any small loose bits of broken shell to neaten the cut edge.

Scoop all the egg out of the halved shells and mash well. Mix in the onion, butter, soured cream and seasoning to taste. Gently press this mixture back into the shells. Smooth the surface with the back of a wetted spoon.

Lightly beat the remaining egg and brush some over the surface of the filling. Coat with breadcrumbs. Brush lightly with more egg and coat with any remaining crumbs. Heat the oil in a frying pan (skillet) and cook the eggs, crumbed side down, until golden. Carefully lift them from the pan and serve in nests of shredded lettuce. Halve or quarter the tomato slices and use to garnish. Serve at once.

# HARE PÂTÉ

Traditionally, game such as venison and hare plays an important role in Polish cooking. This fine pâté would probably be cooked by steaming on the hob rather than in a bain marie in the oven. Serves 12.

---

1 lb/500 g/1 lb belly of pork (fresh pork sides), rind removed

---

2 lb/1 kg/2 lb hare joints

---

2 medium onions, halved

---

2 bay leaves

---

parsley sprig

---

salt and freshly ground black pepper

---

1 tsp ground allspice

---

½ tsp ground ginger

---

freshly grated nutmeg

---

2 cups/75 g/3 oz fresh breadcrumbs

---

1 egg, beaten

---

8 rashers rindless streaky bacon (bacon slices)

---

a little butter

---

Brown the pork in a heavy frying pan (skillet), then transfer it to a large saucepan. Brown the hare joints all over in the fat from the pork. Add the joints to the pork and pour some water into the frying pan. Bring to the boil, stirring, to save all the cooking residue and pour it over the meat. Add the onions, bay leaves and parsley with some pepper and just a little salt.

Pour in enough water to just cover the meat. Bring to the boil, reduce the heat and cover the pan. Simmer for 1 hour. Leave until the meat is just cool enough to handle.

Scoop the onions out of the pan and mince (grind) them or process until smooth in a food processor. Cut all the meat off the hare joints and mince it twice or process until smooth. Cut the pork into chunks and mince it in the same way. Bring the cooking liquid to the boil and boil hard, in the open pan, until reduced to 1¼ cups/300 ml/½ pt – this will take up to 30 minutes, if not longer.

Mix the meats with the onions, spices, breadcrumbs and egg. Strain the reduced liquid through a fine sieve into the pâté and mix well. Add plenty of seasoning – taste a little of the mixture to check for saltiness. Set the oven at 180°C/350°F/gas 4.

Stretch the bacon with the back of a knife, then use it to line a 25 × 10 cm/10 × 4 in loaf tin, overlapping the rashers (slices) slightly. Press the mixture into the tin. Fold the ends of the bacon rashers over the top. Butter a piece of greaseproof (waxed) paper and press it on the pâté, then cover with foil. Place in a roasting tin and pour boiling water around the loaf tin. Bake for 1 hour. Weight the pâté until cool (page 11), then chill overnight. Turn out and serve in slices.

# POTATO DOUGH FINGERS

These are similar to caraway breadsticks but their texture is short rather than crisp. They are quick and easy to make. Makes 40–45.

---

½ lb/225 g/8 oz potato

---

2 cups/225 g/8 oz plain flour (all purpose flour)

---

½ tsp salt

---

½ cup/100 g/4 oz butter

---

2 tsp baking powder

---

2 tsp caraway seeds

---

1 egg, beaten

---

beaten egg to glaze

---

coarse salt to sprinkle (optional)

---

Boil the potato in its skin until tender – about 20 minutes. Drain and cool, then peel. Rub the potato through a sieve.

Set the oven at 200°C/400°F/gas 6. Grease two baking sheets. Sift the flour and salt into a bowl. Rub in the butter, then stir in the baking powder and caraway seeds. Add the potato and egg, then mix to form a soft dough.

Take small portions of dough, about the size of a large cherry, and roll them into 8.5 cm/3½ in fingers. Place slightly apart on the baking sheets and brush with a little beaten egg. Sprinkle the sticks with a little coarse salt, if liked. Bake for about 15 minutes, until golden. Cool on a wire rack.

## CABBAGE AND MUSHROOM ROLLS

These are delicious as a snack or as an accompaniment to soup. This quantity makes 24 rolls.

*1 tsp (active) dried yeast or 15 g/½ oz fresh yeast (½ cake compressed yeast)*

*2 tbsp lukewarm milk*

*1 tsp sugar*

*2 cups/225 g/8 oz strong white flour (hard wheat flour)*

*6 tbsp/75 g/3 oz butter*

*pinch of salt*

*1 egg yolk*

*2 tbsp soured cream*

*beaten egg to glaze*

***FILLING***

*¾ lb/350 g/12 oz green cabbage, trimmed of tough stalk*

*3 dried mushrooms*

*1 small onion, finely chopped*

*2 tbsp/25 g/1 oz butter*

*½ tsp sugar*

*½ tsp vinegar*

*salt and freshly ground black pepper*

Sprinkle the dried yeast over the milk and sugar. Cream the fresh yeast with the milk and sugar. Leave in a warm place until frothy. Sift the flour into a bowl and rub in the butter. Stir in the salt, then make a well in the mixture and add the egg yolk and soured cream. Stir the yeast liquid into the egg and cream, gradually incorporating the dry ingredients. Mix to a soft dough.

Turn out the dough on to a lightly floured surface and knead for about 10 minutes, until it becomes smooth and elastic. Place in a clean bowl, cover with cling film (plastic wrap) and leave in a warm place until doubled in size. This will take 1½–2 hours.

For the filling, cook the cabbage in boiling water for 10 minutes. Place the mushrooms in a small plan and add just enough water to cover. Heat until simmering and cook for 10–15 minutes, until tender. Drain the cabbage well, then squeeze out all the water and chop finely. (A food processor is useful for this.) Drain and chop the mushrooms, saving the liquid to flavour a sauce or soup.

Cook the onion in the butter until soft but not browned – about 10 minutes. Mix the cabbage and mushrooms with the onion, adding the sugar, vinegar and seasoning to taste.

Set the oven at 220°C/425°F/gas 7. Lightly knead the risen dough and divide it in half. Break one portion into 12 equal pieces. Roll a small piece of dough into an oblong measuring about 7.5 × 10 cm/ 3 × 4 in. Use your fingertips to press out the corners of the dough. Mound a teaspoonful of the filling in the middle of the dough, then fold one end over it. Brush the opposite end with a little beaten egg, then

CABBAGE AND
MUSHROOM ROLLS

fold it over to make a neat roll. Place on a greased baking sheet with the join down. Continuing rolling and filling the dough. Leave the rolls to rise in a warm place, loosely covered with cling film (plastic wrap) or plastic, for about 30 minutes. Brush the rolls with beaten egg.

Bake for 10–15 minutes, until golden. Transfer to a wire rack to cool slightly. The rolls are at their best while still hot or warm but they are also perfectly good when cold.

## CANAPÉS

Traditionally, a colourful array of canapés, rather like mini open sandwiches, is served with vodka before a special meal. Thinly sliced rye bread or day-old wholewheat or white bread may be used as the base. Butters or spreads are the first topping and other ingredients are added in an elaborate garnish.

Cut the crusts off the bread, then cut each slice into neat squares or use a biscuit (cookie) cutter to stamp out small rounds. Try some of the following topping suggestions or exercise your imagination by combining cooked meats, fresh herbs, cheese, soured cream and mustard with tiny portions of salad vegetables, such as radish or red and green pepper.

**HERRING SPREAD AND EGG** Top triangles of bread with herring spread (see page 14). Add halved hard-boiled (hard-cooked) egg slices and sprigs of dill for garnish.

**HERRING AND ONION** Cut salted herring fillet across into thin strips. Arrange one or two strips on squares of buttered bread. Top with very fine slices of onion, separated into rings and thin slices of pickled cucumber (dill pickle).

**HERRING AND PICKLED CUCUMBER** Top rounds of buttered bread with a slice of pickled cucumber (dill pickle). Cut rollmops into thin slices and place a slice on each canapé. Top with a tiny dollop of soured cream and a sprig of dill or parsley.

**PÂTÉ AND PICKLED MUSHROOMS** Top small squares of buttered bread with thin slices of hare pâté (page 17). Slice pickled mushrooms (available from delicatessen) and place a slice on each canapé. Add a sprig of parsley to each.

CANAPÉS

**CHEESE AND TOMATO** Top small rounds of buttered bread with cottage cheese spread (page 13) and quartered tomato slices. Sprinkle with chopped chives.

**EWE'S CHEESE WITH CUCUMBER** Top small triangles of buttered bread with thinly sliced cucumber and small dollops of ewe's cheese with paprika (page 13).

**SMOKED SALMON** Top rounds of buttered bread with tiny smoked salmon rolls. Add a little soured cream to each and garnish with quartered lemon slices and dill sprigs.

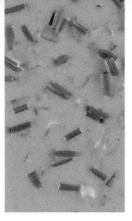

# 2

# SOUPS

As well as being one of the most popular of first courses, served in sophisticated restaurants or as part of any celebration meal, a hearty soup may well constitute a family meal. Good beef stock made from marrow bones, or by boiling an otherwise tough joint, forms the basis for many favourite recipes. Alternatively, veal stock and fish stock may be used. Some of the meat may be left in the soup or, more likely, if it is not eaten as a main course it will all be set aside as a filling for pierogi (page 64) or naleśniki (page 73), or to make Polish schnitzel (page 42). Cabbage and mushroom rolls (page 18) or potato dough fingers (page 17) are typical accompaniments for soup.

Beetreet soup (barszcz) is one of the best known of Polish soups. Traditionally, it is served as part of the Christmas eve meal. For that occasion, when meat is avoided, the soup is prepared using fish stock. Tiny mushroom-filled dumplings – uzska (page 62) – are served as an accompaniment.

As well as savoury soups, Poland is renowned for fruit soups made using plums, cherries, apples or other fruits in season. These may be served hot or cold, as a first course or as a light meal on their own just like savoury soup. Plaited bread (page 70) or buchty (page 70) may be offered with fruit soups.

BEETROOT SOUP

## BEETROOT (BEET) SOUP

Known as Barszcz (pronounced Barstch), beetroot (beet) soup has a naturally sweet flavour. This is one of the dishes served as part of the traditional, 12-course Christmas eve meal, when uska (page 62) are an essential accompaniment. Meat is not eaten on Christmas eve, so fish stock (see page 15) would be used in place of beef stock. Serves 6.

*1 onion, roughly chopped*

*1 leek, sliced*

*piece of celeriac (about ¼ lb/100 g/4 oz) or 2 celery sticks, cut into pieces*

*a little fat or oil*

*2½ cups/225 g/8 oz cabbage, shredded*

*500 g/1 lb raw beetroot (beet), peeled and grated.*

*1 bay leaf*

*1 tbsp allspice berries*

*7½ cups/1.75 litres/3 pt beef stock (page 27)*

*salt and freshly ground black pepper*

*3 tbsp fermented beetroot (beet) juice or 1–2 tsp cider vinegar*

*uzska (page 62) to serve (optional)*

Brown the onion, leek and celeriac in the minimum of fat in a large, heavy-based saucepan. Stir frequently to prevent the vegetables from sticking. Add the cabbage, beetroot (beet), bay leaf and allspice, mixing well. Pour in the stock and add a little seasoning. Bring to the boil and reduce the heat so that the soup simmers steadily. Cover and cook for 1 hour.

Strain the soup through a fine sieve. Return it to the rinsed pan and add the fermented beetroot juice with seasoning to taste. If using cider vinegar, add just enough to quell the sweetness of the beetroot rather than creating a sweet-sour flavour. Heat through and serve with uzska, if liked.

Note: to make clear beetroot (beet) soup, reduce the quantity of flavouring vegetables (other than beetroot) by half. Use a clear stock. Strain, then clarify the soup (page 27) before serving.

## KRUPNIK

This soup is made of grain – barley usually, or buckwheat may be used – and has the same name as a potent drink made from caramel, honey, spices and Polish spirit. If you want to try making the drink, read the note below; here I shall concentrate on the soup.

---

*1 onion, chopped*

*2 carrots, diced*

*1 leek, sliced*

*2 tbsp/25 g/1 oz fat*

*5 cups/1.15 L/2 pt beef stock (page 27)*

*½ cup/100 g/4 oz pearl barley*

*salt and freshly ground black pepper*

*1 bay leaf*

*½ small celeriac, diced*

---

Cook the onion, carrots and leek in the fat in a large saucepan, until slightly softened but not browned. Pour in the stock, then add the barley with a sprinkling of seasoning and the bay leaf. Bring to the boil, reduce the heat and cover the pan. Simmer for 30 minutes.

Add the celeriac to the soup, give it a good stir and re-cover the pan. Simmer the soup for a further 30 minutes by which time the barley should be plump and tender. Taste for seasoning before serving. This soup should be served freshly cooked otherwise the barley swells and absorbs all the liquid.

**KRUPNIK: THE DRINK** Heat ½ cup/100 g/4 oz sugar with 4 tbsp water until the sugar has dissolved, stirring occasionally. Bring to the boil and boil hard until the syrup turns to a golden caramel. Off the heat, add 4 tbsp boiling water – take care as the caramel spits furiously when water is added. Add 1 cinnamon stick, 10 allspice berries, 10 black peppercorns and ½ tsp aniseeds. Stir well, then heat gently until the caramel boils. Set aside to cool slightly. Strain the spiced caramel, return it to the pan and add ⅓ cup/100 g/4 oz clear honey. Heat, stirring, until combined. Cool slightly. Gradually stir in ⅔ cup/150 ml/¼ pt Polish spirit. Serve at once, while still hot, or allow to cool before serving.

## SAUERKRAUT SOUP

Kapusniak by name, here is another of Poland's popular soups. For authenticity, add all the juices from the sauerkraut to give the soup a sour flavour. However, if you are unused to the tang of authentic Polish dishes, squeeze out the sauerkraut as I have done in this recipe. Serves 4–6.

| |
|---|
| ½ lb/225 g/8 oz belly of pork (fresh pork sides), rind removed |
| 1 large onion, chopped |
| 1 leek, thinly sliced |
| 1 carrot, diced |
| 5 cups/1.15 L/2 pt stock, such as beef, chicken or veal |
| ¾ lb/350 g/12 oz sauerkraut |
| 1 potato, diced |
| salt and freshly ground black pepper |

Dice the pork, then cook it over a low heat in a large, heavy-based saucepan until the fat runs. Add the onion and leek. Continue to cook, stirring frequently, until the onion is slightly softened but not browned. Stir in the carrot and pour in the stock, then bring to the boil. Reduce the heat, cover and simmer for 30 minutes.

Drain the sauerkraut, reserving the juice, and squeeze out all the remaining juice. Use a sharp knife to slice across the pat of squeezed sauerkraut. Add the sauerkraut to the soup with the potato and some seasoning. Stir well and simmer, covered, for a further 30 minutes.

Taste and adjust the seasoning. Stir in some or all of the juice reserved from the sauerkraut, according to taste. Serve piping hot.

PRETTY WOODEN BIRDS
FOR SALE.

POTATO SOUP

## POTATO SOUP

This delicious soup is a treat for garlic lovers. It is wonderfully full-flavoured and warming; if it was any less satisfying I'm sure I would have consumed the whole pot full when I made it.

| |
|---|
| 9 slices/175 g/6 oz rindless smoked bacon, diced |
| 2 large cloves garlic, crushed |
| 1 leek, sliced |
| 1½ lb/675 g/1½ lb potatoes, cut into 2.5 cm/1 in cubes |
| 3¾ cups/900 ml/1½ pt stock, such as beef, veal or chicken (page 27) |
| salt and freshly ground black pepper |
| 2 tbsp chopped fresh parsley or dill |

Place the bacon in a large, heavy-based saucepan and heat gently until the fat runs. Add the garlic and leek and cook, stirring occasionally, until the leek is slightly softened.

Stir in the potatoes and stock, then add some seasoning. Bring to the boil and cook at a good simmer, with the pan half covered, for about 15 minutes. The soup is ready when the potatoes are just beginning to break up – give it a good stir and the liquid will thicken slightly but there should still be pieces of potato left. Sprinkle in the parsley or dill and serve at once.

## DRIED MUSHROOM SOUP

Dried mushrooms are expensive but they make a superb soup. In some households this special mushroom soup would be served as an alternative to beetroot (beet) soup on Christmas eve; however water would be used instead of beef stock. Serves 4.

½ oz/15 g/½ oz dried mushrooms

2½ cups/600 ml/1 pt water

1 onion, very finely chopped

a little fat or butter

3 tbsp plain flour (all purpose flour)

1¼ cups/300 ml/½ pt beef stock (page 27)

salt and freshly ground black pepper

1¼ cups/300 ml/½ pt soured cream

2 tbsp snipped chives

Place the mushrooms and water in a saucepan and heat gently until simmering. Cover and simmer for 5 minutes. Lift out the mushrooms with a slotted spoon. Press excess liquid from them and chop finely. Strain the cooking liquor through muslin (cheesecloth) and reserve.

Cook the onion in the minimum of fat in a saucepan over low heat for about 10 minutes, until soft but not browned. Stir in the flour, then slowly add the stock, stirring all the time. Pour in the reserved mushroom liquor, add the mushrooms and stir well. Bring to a simmer, cover and cook for 30 minutes.

Taste and season the soup, then stir in the soured cream and heat gently for a few minutes without boiling. Serve sprinkled with chives.

DRIED MUSHROOM SOUP

## CHLODNIK

Chlodnik is a summery soup, made when the beetroot (beet) are very young and their leaves are tender. In Poland, soured milk – made by adding a culture as when making soured cream – is used instead of the combination of yogurt and soured cream which I include. Serves 4–6.

1 small onion, finely chopped

1 clove garlic, crushed (optional)

a little fat or butter

½ lb/225 g/8 oz young beetroot (beet) leaves, Swiss chard or spinach, shredded

1¼ cups/300 ml/½ pt veal or chicken stock (page 27)

1 cucumber, peeled and thinly sliced (about 1 lb/500 g/1 lb in weight)

2 tsp sugar

1 tbsp lemon juice

salt and freshly ground black pepper

1¼ cups/300 ml/½ pt natural yogurt

1¼ cups/300 ml/½ pt soured cream

4 eggs, hard-boiled (hard-cooked) and roughly chopped

4 small beetroot (beet), cooked, peeled and roughly chopped

2 tbsp chopped fresh dill

2 tbsp snipped chives

Cook the onion and garlic in the minimum of fat in a large saucepan for about 10–15 minutes over low heat, until very soft but not browned. Stir in the shredded leaves and pour in the stock. Bring to the boil, reduce the heat and cover the pan. Simmer for 15 minutes, or until the leaves are tender. Leave to cool, then chill.

Stir in the cucumber, sugar, lemon juice and seasoning. Add the yogurt and soured cream, stir well and taste for seasoning. Extra lemon juice may be added if liked. Ladle the soup into bowls, add the eggs, beetroot (beet) and herbs, then serve at once.

## ZUREK

This is a vegetable soup which is thickened and soured with fermented rye or oat flour. The fermented liquid is known as zur. This must be prepared three days in advance. Serves 4–6.

½ cup/50 g/2 oz rye flour

1 cup/250 ml/8 fl oz water

the end crust of a rye loaf

2 cloves garlic, crushed

9 slices/175 g/6 oz smoked rindless streaky bacon, diced

1 onion, finely chopped

2 celery sticks, thinly sliced

2 carrots, diced

1 leek, sliced

1 parsnip, diced

1½ cups/100 g/4 oz green cabbage, shredded

1 bay leaf

½ tsp ground allspice

5 cups/1.15 L/2 pt good beef stock (page 27)

salt and freshly ground black pepper

⅔ cup/150 ml/¼ pt soured cream (optional)

2 tbsp chopped fresh parsley

Make the zur three days before preparing the soup: mix the flour with the water and crust in a perfectly clean large jar. Stir in the garlic. Cover the jar with muslin (cheesecloth) or absorbent kitchen paper and secure with an elastic band. Leave in a warm place for three days. Stir the mixture every day. It should smell strongly of garlic and have a slightly soured tang, which is sharp rather than unpleasant. If there is any trace of a nasty odour, then discard the mixture.

To make the soup, heat the bacon in a large, heavy-based saucepan until the fat runs, then continue to cook until the pieces are crisp and brown. Use a slotted spoon to remove the bacon and set aside. Add all the vegetables, except the parsnip and cabbage, to the fat remaining in the pan and cook, stirring frequently, for 10 minutes. Add the parsnip, cabbage, bay leaf and spice. Pour in the stock and season, then bring to the boil. Reduce the heat, cover the pan and simmer for 15–30 minutes, depending on how well cooked you like your vegetables.

Strain the zur into the soup and bring to the boil, stirring all the time. Simmer for 10–15 minutes. Taste and adjust the seasoning, then stir in the soured cream if used. Serve topped with chopped parsley.

## PEA SOUP

Sliced kabanos are tasty in this delicious soup, added after sieving or blending. Serves 4.

1 onion, roughly chopped

1 clove garlic, crushed

1 bay leaf

a little fat or butter

1 lb/500 g/1 lb frozen peas or shelled fresh peas

3¾ cups/900 ml/1½ pt stock such as ham, beef, veal or chicken (page 27)

1 small potato, diced

salt and freshly ground black pepper

⅔ cup/150 ml/¼ pt soured cream

Cook the onion, garlic and bay leaf in a little fat in a saucepan over low heat until soft but not browned – about 10 minutes. Add the peas, pour in the stock and stir in the potato. Sprinkle in a little seasoning. Bring to the boil, reduce the heat, cover and simmer for 30 minutes.

Sieve or blend the soup until smooth. Return it to the pan and heat through. Taste for seasoning, stir in the soured cream and serve at once.

## PLUM SOUP

This soup is spicy and full-bodied, good hot as well as cold. Served sliced and toasted buchty (page 70) as an accompaniment. Serves 6.

1½ lb/675 g/1½ lb plums

2½ cups/600 ml/1 pt water

4 cloves

4 allspice berries

1 cinnamon stick

½–¾ cup/100–175 g/4–6 oz sugar

1 tbsp arrowroot

1¼ cups/300 ml/½ pt red wine

⅔ cup/150 ml/¼ pt soured cream

Simmer the plums in the water with all the spices added in a saucepan for 1 hour. Make sure that the fruit cooks very gently all the time and keep the pan closely covered. Cool slightly. Discard the cinnamon stick and rub the fruit through a sieve, discarding the other whole spices.

Heat the sieved fruit and the sugar in the rinsed pan until the sugar has dissolved. Add the smaller quantity of sugar first, then taste the soup and add more if necessary. Blend the arrowroot with a little of the wine. Stir in the remaining wine, then pour the mixture into the soup and bring to the boil, stirring. Remove the pan from the heat as soon as the soup boils.

Ladle into dishes and swirl soured cream into the soup.

## CHERRY SOUP

This is a delicate and refreshing chilled soup. Serves 4.

1½ lb/675 g/1½ lb cherries, stalks removed

1 cinnamon stick

2½ cups/600 ml/1 pt water plus 2 tbsp

½ cup/100 g/4 oz sugar

2 tbsp arrowroot

⅔ cup/150 ml/¼ pt soured cream

Put 1 lb/500 g/1 lb of the cherries in a saucepan with the cinnamon stick and all but the 2 tbsp water. Bring to the boil, reduce the heat and cover. Simmer the fruit for 30 minutes, then cool slightly. Stone (pit) the reserved cherries.

Discard the cinnamon stick and press the cherries through a sieve, with all the cooking liquid. Pour the sieved fruit back into the rinsed pan. Add the sugar and reserved cherries. Heat, stirring, until the sugar has dissolved. Blend the arrowroot to a smooth paste with the remaining water. Add a little of the hot soup, then pour the mixture into the pan of soup and bring to the boil, stirring. As soon as the soup is boiling, remove the pan from the heat and cool slightly. Whisk in the soured cream and cover the surface of the soup with cling film (plastic wrap) or greaseproof (waxed) paper. Cool and chill.

Stir the soup well before serving, ladled into delicate soup dishes or glass dishes.

## BEEF STOCK

Ask the butcher for marrow bones – one of the few purchases that may be made cheaply! Remember to have them chopped into pieces that will fit into a saucepan.

*beef marrow bones (enough to three-quarters fill your largest saucepan)*

*1 large onion*

*2 carrots, cut into chunks*

*1 leek, cut into chunks*

*2 bay leaves*

*a few large parsley sprigs*

*6 black peppercorns*

Set the oven at 220°C/420°F/gas 7. Put the bones in a roasting tin. Bake for 45–60 minutes, until browned. The cooking time and temperature is not important but the bones should be browned – put them in the bottom of the oven when you are baking or if you are cooking another meal.

Drain off all the fat and put the bones in a large saucepan. Wash the onion, trim off roots and loose peel but do not remove all the peel. Quarter it and add the pieces to the pan. The onion peel adds both colour and flavour to the stock. Add the carrots, leek, herbs and peppercorns. Pour in cold water to cover, bring to the boil and reduce the heat. Skim off any scum, then cover and simmer for 3 hours, topping up with boiling water occasionally to keep the bones covered.

Cool, then strain the stock. Pour it back into the pan and boil, uncovered, for 20 minutes to reduce it slightly and concentrate the flavour. If it is to be frozen, boil the stock until it is greatly reduced and concentrated, then water may be added on thawing, before use.

**TO CLARIFY STOCK OR SOUP** Strain the stock through a fine sieve. Scald a piece of muslin (cheesecloth) and a sieve. Pour the stock into a clean pan and whisk in 2 egg whites with their crushed shells for every 3¾ cups/900 ml/1½ pints stock. Whisk the stock over medium heat until it has a thick froth on the surface. Stop whisking and allow the stock to boil up. Turn the gas down or lift the pan off the heat, allowing the crust to subside. Repeat once or twice more before straining the stock through a muslin-lined sieve. The process should be repeated until the stock or soup is sparkling clear.

**VEAL STOCK** Use veal bones instead of beef bones. The bones may be roasted or used uncooked to make a lighter stock.

**CHICKEN STOCK** Use a meaty chicken carcass left from a roast or 2 chicken quarters instead of the beef bones. Do not roast either first.

CHERRY SOUP

# 3

# FISH

Only a small area of Poland, at the north of the country, has access to a coast, so fresh sea fish is rarely available in the majority of areas. Instead salted herrings are popular and canned fish is put to a number of uses. Fresh water fish, such as trout, carp and pike, are prized instead of salt water specimens.

Fish is eaten on the important fast days in the religious calendar, most significantly on Christmas eve when carp forms the centrepiece of the traditional twelve-course menu. To some extent the methods for preparing fish reflect the Jewish influence on Polish cooking. Fish in aspic, fishballs and stuffed fish are all popular.

Among the old recipes it is not difficult to find methods for making elaborate soups using vast quantities of crayfish, or others calling for lobster from the sea. However, such extravagant creations are remnants from the great kitchens of the country and they are not easy to find in the restaurants or private kitchens of modern Poland. This chapter offers a taste of the more practical recipes that are likely to appeal to the contemporary palate and average purse.

FISHBALLS

## FISHBALLS

These fishballs may be served as part of a salad, as below, or they may be served hot, coated with horseradish sauce made in the same way as in the previous recipe (fish with horseradish sauce). Serves 4.

*1 small onion, finely chopped*

*2 tbsp/25 g/1 oz butter*

*⅔ cup/25 g/1 oz fresh white breadcrumbs*

*¾ lb/350 g/12 oz cod fillet, skinned*

*1 egg white*

*2 tbsp chopped fresh dill*

*salt and freshly ground white pepper*

*3¾ cups/900 ml/1½ pt fish stock*

*white part of 1 leek, thinly sliced*

*1 lettuce heart, shredded*

*¼ cucumber, thinly sliced (about ¼ lb/100 g/4 oz)*

*8 radishes, sliced*

*6 tbsp mayonnaise*

*6 tbsp soured cream*

*dill sprigs to garnish*

Cook the onion in the butter for about 10 minutes, until soft but not browned. Mix with the breadcrumbs in a bowl. Mince (grind) the fish or purée it in a food processor and add it to the crumb mixture. Stir in the egg white, dill and plenty of seasoning.

Using clean hands, wet them and roll small portions of the fish mixture into walnut-sized balls. The mixture should make 16 balls. Heat the fish stock in a saucepan until simmering. Add the fishballs and simmer for 10 minutes. Drain and cool.

Blanch the leek in boiling water for 30–60 seconds, drain immediately and rinse under cold water. Drain and pat dry on absorbent kitchen paper. Arrange the lettuce, leek and cucumber on individual plates or on one platter. Group the fishballs on the salad, adding the radish slices for colour.

Mix the mayonnaise and soured cream with a little seasoning to taste. Spoon this dressing over the fishballs. Garnish with dill and serve.

## CHRISTMAS EVE CARP

Poached carp with a sweet-sour sauce, enriched with almonds and raisins, is the old fashioned main course for the 12-course Christmas eve meal. However, this sauce is not to every Westerner's taste and it has also been replaced by alternatives in many Polish households. Horseradish sauce or a platter of poached fish dressed in aspic may be served instead of this sauce, which is something of an acquired taste. Here I have adapted the ingredients for the sauce, substituting water for fish stock as I found this gave a better taste to the end result. The sauce without fish stock is a rich, red wine sauce.

Traditionally, so Małgosia tells me, the live carp was brought home a few days before Christmas and kept in a tank of water – or even the bath – until the day on which it was to be killed and eaten. If carp is not available, poach a whole grey mullet instead, or serve cod or haddock fillets coated with the sauce. Serves 6.

| |
|---|
| 3 lb/1.5 kg/3 lb carp, gutted and descaled |
| 7½ cups/1.75 L/3 pt fish stock |
| 1 onion, finely chopped |
| 1 bay leaf |
| 4 tbsp/50 g/2 oz butter |
| 6 tbsp/40 g/1½ oz plain flour (all purpose flour) |
| 1¼ cups/300 ml/½ pt water |
| 1¼ cups/300 ml/½ pt red wine |
| about 2 tbsp demerara sugar |
| about 2 tbsp lemon juice |
| ⅓ cup/40 g/1½ oz blanched almonds, cut into slivers |
| 2 tbsp/25 g/1 oz raisins |
| salt and freshly ground black pepper |

**GARNISH**

| |
|---|
| parsley sprigs |
| 1 lemon, cut into wedges |

Tie string around the body of the fish in two or three places to keep it in a neat shape as it cooks. Place the fish in a fish kettle or large roasting tin and pour in the stock. Heat until simmering, cover and cook gently for 30 minutes, until the fish is cooked through.

Lift the fish from the cooking liquid. Remove the skin and transfer the fish to a serving platter. Cover with foil and keep hot.

Make the sauce while the fish is poaching. Cook the onion and bay leaf in half the butter for about 15 minutes, until very soft but not browned. Stir in the flour, then gradually pour in the water and wine, stirring all the time. Bring to the boil and simmer for 3 minutes. Stir in the sugar, lemon juice, almonds and raisins. Taste the sauce and add seasoning, adding a little extra lemon juice or sugar to achieve the right balance of sweet to sour for your taste. Stir in the remaining butter.

Spoon a little of the sauce over the fish, then serve the remainder separately. Garnish the sauced fish with parsley and lemon wedges before serving.

## POACHED TROUT

A simple method for serving delicate, pink-fleshed trout. Serves 4.

| |
|---|
| 4 trout, cleaned with heads on |
| 2½ cups/600 ml/1 pt water |
| 1 small onion, sliced |
| 1 bay leaf |
| parsley sprig |
| salt and freshly ground black pepper |
| ¼ cup/50 g/2 oz butter |

**GARNISH**

| |
|---|
| 2 eggs, hard-boiled (hard-cooked) and chopped |
| 1 tbsp chopped fresh dill |

Rinse and dry the trout. Pour the water into a large shallow pan and add the onion, bay leaf, parsley and seasoning. Heat gently until simmering, then cook for 5 minutes.

Reduce the heat so that the liquid barely simmers and add the trout. Cook very gently for 5–7 minutes, turning the trout over once, until cooked through. Meanwhile, melt the butter in a small saucepan.

Transfer the trout to a warmed serving platter. Carefully remove the skin using the point of a knife. Turn each fish over and remove the skin from the second side. Pour the hot butter over and garnish with chopped egg. Sprinkle with dill and serve at once.

MARINATED FISH

## MARINATED FISH

Use the freshest possible fish. If you are using mackerel look for small, young specimens that tend to be fine-flaked and not over rich. The fish rolls may be served with boiled potatoes and beetroot salad, or accompanied by rye bread. Serves 4.

| |
| --- |
| *2½ cups/600 ml/1 pt water* |
| *1 bay leaf* |
| *1 onion, thinly sliced* |
| *salt and freshly ground black pepper* |
| *2 tbsp vinegar* |
| *4 mackerel or herrings, cleaned with heads off* |
| *1 small carrot* |
| *1 pickled cucumber (dill pickle)* |
| ***GARNISH*** |
| *1 pickled cucumber (dill pickle), sliced* |
| *dill sprigs* |

Simmer the water, bay leaf, onion and seasoning for 10 minutes with a close-fitting lid on the pan. Add the vinegar and cool.

Bone the fish: lay each one flesh side down on a board and press firmly down the middle of the bone. Turn the fish over and the main bone should lift off easily, bringing with it most of the small bones at the side. Pick off all remaining bones. Cut each fish in half lengthways to give eight fillets.

Cut eight thin sticks from the carrot and blanch them in boiling water for 1 minute. Drain and rinse under cold water. Cut eight thin sticks lengthways from the pickled cucumber (dill pickle). Place a stick of carrot and pickled cucumber at the wide end of each fish fillet and roll up to the tail, then secure with wooden cocktail sticks (toothpicks). Place in the prepared, cooled liquid. Heat very gently until the liquid is steaming but not simmering. Cover and leave at this heat for 10 minutes. Remove from the heat and leave the fish to cool completely in the liquid. The rolls should be cooked through by the time they have cooled.

Lift the fish rolls from the cooking liquid when cool. Serve garnished with pickled cucumber and dill, whole or chopped.

FISH IN HORSERADISH SAUCE

## FISH IN HORSERADISH SAUCE

This simple dish of cod in a creamy horseradish sauce is quite delicious. Serves 4.

*1 lb / 500 g / 1 lb cod fillet, skinned and cut into four portions*

*2 bay leaves*

*salt and freshly ground black pepper*

*1 cup / 250 ml / 8 fl oz water*

*2 tbsp / 25 g / 1 oz butter*

*¼ cup / 25 g / 1 oz plain flour (all purpose flour)*

*3 tbsp grated horseradish*

*1¼ cups / 300 ml / ½ pt soured cream*

***GARNISH***

*dill or parsley sprigs*

*lemon slices*

Place the fish in a shallow pan and add the bay leaves. Sprinkle with seasoning, pour in the water and heat gently until simmering. Cook gently for 3–5 minutes, until the fish is just cooked. Use a fish slice to transfer the pieces of fish to an ovenproof dish. Strain the fish cooking liquor and reserve.

Set the oven at 220°C/425°F/gas 7. Melt the butter in a small saucepan and stir in the flour. Gradually pour the reserved fish cooking liquor on to the flour mixture, stirring all the time. Add the horseradish and bring to the boil to make a very thick sauce. Stir in a little seasoning and the soured cream. Spoon the sauce over the fish.

Bake for about 10 minutes, until the sauce is just beginning to brown. Garnish with dill and lemon, then serve at once.

# HERRING AND BEAN SALAD

Dried beans are used in a variety of ways, to make soups, in stews or cold in salads as here. Serves 4.

| |
|---|
| *1 cup/175 g/6 oz dried butter beans (dried fava or lima beans), soaked overnight in cold water to cover* |
| *salt and freshly ground black pepper* |
| *4 salted herring fillets* |
| *2 tbsp olive oil* |
| *1 medium potato, cooked and diced* |
| *1 pickled cucumber (dill pickle), sliced* |
| *½ cup/50 g/2 oz shelled peas, cooked* |
| *4 tbsp soured cream* |
| *4 tbsp mayonnaise* |
| *2 tbsp chopped fresh dill or parsley* |
| *2 tbsp finely chopped onion* |
| *1 tsp grated lemon rind* |
| *lemon wedges to garnish* |

Drain the soaked beans. Cook them in plenty of fresh, boiling water for 1 hour, until tender. Add salt to the water half way through cooking. Drain well and cool.

Cut the herring fillets into strips and mix with the cooled beans and olive oil. Add the potato, pickled cucumber (dill pickle) and peas, mixing lightly to avoid breaking up the ingredients. Transfer to individual bowls or a large dish.

Mix the soured cream, mayonnaise, dill, onion, lemon rind and seasoning to taste. Spoon this dressing over the salad and add lemon wedges to garnish. The dressing should be tossed into the ingredients just before the salad is eaten. Lemon juice may be squeezed over to sharpen the salad.

TRADITIONAL POLISH FESTIVITIES

# FRIED FISH WITH MUSHROOM SAUCE

One dried mushroom is sufficient to flavour a tempting sauce that enlivens plain cooked fish. Serves 4.

| |
|---|
| *4 herrings or small mackerel, gutted with heads off* |
| *4 tbsp plain flour (all purpose flour)* |
| *salt and freshly ground black pepper* |
| *4 tbsp oil* |
| ***SAUCE*** |
| *1 large dried mushroom* |
| *1¼ cups/300 ml/½ pt water* |
| *1 onion, finely chopped* |
| *2 tbsp/25 g/1 oz butter* |
| *3 tbsp plain flour (all purpose flour)* |
| *⅔ cup/150 ml/¼ pt soured cream* |
| ***GARNISH*** |
| *8 thin lemon wedges* |
| *4 dill or parsley sprigs* |

Bone the fish as described in the recipe for marinated fish (page 31). Coat in the flour and plenty of seasoning, then set aside.

For the sauce, simmer the mushroom in the water, covered, for 5 minutes. Lift the mushroom from the liquor and chop finely. Gently cook the onion in the butter in a small pan for about 10 minutes until well cooked but not browned. Stir in the flour, then gradually add the mushroom liquor, stirring all the time. Bring to the boil and add the chopped mushroom. Season the sauce, simmer for 1 minute, then stir in the soured cream. Keep warm but do not allow to boil.

Heat the oil in a frying pan (skillet) and cook the fish until well browned on both sides. Drain on absorbent kitchen paper before transferring to a warmed serving platter or four plates. Pour a little of the sauce over the fish and serve the rest separately. Garnish with lemon and dill, then serve immediately.

## SMOKED EEL SALAD

Smoked eel makes a tasty salad which may be
served with vegetables – try cucumber salad
(page 59) and boiled new potatoes – or with
thinly sliced rye bread. Serves 4.

*½ lb / 225 g / 8 oz smoked eel fillet*

*4 small tomatoes, thinly sliced*

*2 tbsp finely chopped onion*

*1 tbsp vinegar*

*1 tsp sugar*

*2 tsp water*

*1 small lettuce heart, shredded*

*salt and freshly ground black pepper*

*4 tbsp soured cream*

*a little paprika*

Cut each piece of eel in half lengthways and
pick out all the bones. Arrange the strips of eel
on individual plates with the tomato slices.
Sprinkle the onion over the tomato.

Stir the vinegar, sugar and water together
until the sugar has dissolved. Toss this dressing
with the lettuce and seasoning to taste.
Arrange the lettuce on the plates. Top the
fillets of eel with a little soured cream and
sprinkle with paprika.

# 4

# MEAT, POULTRY AND GAME

Traditionally the Poles are great meat eaters, consuming generous portions as the main part of the meal. Along with its European neighbours, Poland is renowned for hunting traditions, for venison and other game, including wild boar. Pork is a popular meat and it is more readily available than some other types. Veal is greatly favoured but not necessarily easy to find, beef is featured in many recipes and poultry such as chicken or duck is roasted or braised.

Hearty meat stews reflect the harsh climate of the country, providing wholesome mixtures of vegetables and bubbling hot stock or sauce to combat the exterior chill. Boiled meat is also a practical dish that provides an excellent liquor for soup as well as meat to serve with sauce and leftovers to be used as a filling for tasty dumplings. Before roasting, joints are usually marinated in a mixture of fresh vegetables, seasoning and water with vinegar added to tenderize and flavour the meat.

A selection of traditional and popular recipes feature in this chapter, from a roast fillet of beef that would grace affluent tables to famous bigos, the stew that once was the hunter's feast.

BIGOS

## BIGOS

Among the best known of Polish dishes, Bigos is a
meat stew with sausage, sauerkraut and cabbage.
Since it is traditionally a hunter's recipe, the meat
used in the stew may be anything, from wild boar to
hare, rabbit, venison or game birds. I have used pork
but joints of hare or rabbit, cubes of braising venison,
joints of pheasant or even beef may be used. Indeed, a
combination of different meats, including leftover
roasts, may be added. Polish sausage contributes a
wonderful smoked, garlic flavour to the stew. Serve
with potatoes or chunks of rye bread – delicious!
Serves 6.

1 lb / 500 g / 1 lb pork, cubed

12 slices / 225 g / 8 oz smoked rindless streaky bacon, diced

2 onions, sliced

2 bay leaves

2 cloves garlic, crushed

1 lb / 500 g / 1 lb sauerkraut, drained

1 lb / 500 g / 1 lb wiejska sausage, cut into chunks

1 cup / 250 ml / 8 fl oz red wine or stock

2 dried mushrooms or 1 cup / 100 g / 4 oz mushrooms, sliced

salt and freshly ground black pepper

1 lb / 500 g / 1 lb green or white cabbage, trimmed and
shredded

2 tbsp plain flour (all purpose flour)

2 tsbp water

Cook the pork and bacon together in a large, heavy-based flameproof casserole until the fat runs and the cubes of pork are lightly browned. Stir frequently at first to prevent the meat sticking. Add the onions, bay leaves and garlic and cook, stirring, for 5 minutes until the onions are slightly softened.

Squeeze all the liquid from the sauerkraut, then cut across the pat of vegetable to shred it finely. Add to the meat with the sausage and wine or stock. If using dried mushrooms, simmer them in just enough water to cover for 5 minutes. Strain the liquor into the stew and chop the mushrooms. Add the mushrooms and seasoning, then heat until simmering. Cover and simmer for 1 hour, stirring occasionally, until the meat is tender.

Cook the cabbage in boiling salted water for 2 minutes, then drain well. Blend the flour with the water, stir the paste into the stew and bring to the boil, stirring. Cook, uncovered, to evaporate any excess liquid for about 5 minutes. Stir in the cabbage, heat for 1–2 minutes and serve.

Bigos should be juicy but not too wet. Its flavour improves with keeping, so it is ideal for making a day in advance. Make sure the stew is thoroughly heated through before serving. If liked, cook and add the cabbage at the last minute instead of leaving it overnight.

## BOILED BEEF WITH HORSERADISH SAUCE

The stock from the beef makes wonderful soup. Any leftovers from the joint may be minced (ground) for making Polish schnitzel (page 42) or for filling pierogi (page 64). Authentically, the horseradish sauce should be very hot, laden with plenty of fresh horseradish. I have used enough to give the sauce plenty of bite without allowing it to peel the roof off

AUTUMN IN WARSAW'S LAZIENKI PARK.

your mouth. However, if you are unsure of your liking for horseradish it is a good idea to taste the sauce before adding the full amount. Serve boiled potatoes, carrots, green beans or other fresh seasonal vegetables with the meat. Beetroot (beet) and salad with horseradish (page 58), sauerkraut with mushrooms (page 54), carrot and potato hotpot (page 56) or cucumber salad (page 59) are alternative accompaniments. Serves 8.

2¼ lb/1 kg/2¼ lb joint of rolled (fresh) brisket

a little fat

1 carrot, sliced

1 large onion, sliced

1 dried mushroom or the stock from simmering dried mushrooms

1 leek, sliced

large piece of celeriac (about ¼ lb/100 g/4 oz)

1 clove garlic, crushed

1 bay leaf

2 large parsley sprigs

3 tsp salt

freshly ground black pepper

1 tsp allspice berries

**HORSERADISH SAUCE**

2 tbsp/25 g/1 oz butter

¼ cup/25 g/1 oz plain flour (all purpose flour)

4 tbsp grated horseradish

1¼ cups/300 ml/½ pt soured cream

In a large, heavy-based saucepan, brown the joint of meat all over in a little fat – beef dripping is ideal. Add all the vegetables, garlic, herbs and salt, then pour in enough water to just cover the joint of meat. Bring to the boil and skim any scum off the surface. Reduce the heat, cover and simmer for 3 hours, until the meat is very tender.

For the sauce, melt the butter in a pan and stir in the flour. Stir in 1¼ cups/300 ml/½ pt of the beef cooking liquid and the horseradish. Bring to the boil to make a thick sauce, stirring all the time. Simmer for 3 minutes, then stir in the soured cream and season to taste. Heat through until just simmering.

Serve the beef carved into slices, with some of the horseradish sauce poured over. Offer the remaining sauce separately.

## FILLET OF BEEF WITH NOODLES

This is one of Eva's favourite recipes – it is rather expensive but quite mouthwatering. Serves 6.

| |
|---|
| *2 cups/225 g/8 oz plain (all purpose) flour* |
| *salt and freshly ground black pepper* |
| *1 egg, beaten* |
| *1 tbsp water* |
| *2½ lb/1.25 kg/2½ lb fillet of beef, tied in a neat shape* |
| *a little beef dripping or butter* |
| *⅔ cup/150 ml/¼ pt water* |
| *1 dried mushroom or 2 large open mushrooms, sliced, and 1 tbsp mushroom ketchup* |
| *1¼ cups/300 ml/½ pt soured cream* |
| *chopped fresh dill to garnish (optional)* |

First make the noodles: sift the flour and ½ tsp salt into a bowl. Make a well in the middle, then add the egg and water. Mix the flour with the egg to make a firm, quite dry dough. Knead this thoroughly until smooth – the dough will soften and become more pliable as you knead it. Wrap the dough in cling film (plastic wrap) and leave for 15 minutes.

Set the oven at 220°C/425°F/gas 7. Rub the beef all over with seasoning and smear a little beef dripping or butter over the top of the joint. Roast the meat for 40–60 minutes, depending on personal taste. The outside of the joint should be well browned; after 40 minutes the inside will still be bloody, after 60 minutes just the very centre of the joint will be nicely pink and juicy.

Cut the dough in half. Roll out one piece thinly on a lightly floured surface to a square measuring about 25–30 cm/10–12 in. Dust the top of the dough very lightly with flour, fold it in half, dust again and fold in half. Place the folded dough on a board and use a sharp knife to cut strips (across the folds working from one end) measuring slightly less than 1 cm/ 1½ in in width. Shake the noodles free with your fingertips, dust them very lightly with flour and drop them loosely on to a plate. Repeat with the remaining dough. Cook the noodles in a large pan of boiling salted water for about 3 minutes, until just tender but with a little bite. Drain well and toss with a little melted butter, then place on a warmed meat platter. Slice the beef and arrange the slices on the noodles. Cover and keep hot.

Add the water and dried or fresh mushrooms (with ketchup) to the beef cooking juices and simmer for 5 minutes, stirring all the time to scrape the cooking residue off the pan. If using fresh mushrooms, boil the liquid to reduce it slightly as the mushrooms yield liquid. Lift the dried mushroom from the pan, chop it and return to the sauce. Stir in the soured cream and heat gently. Taste for seasoning and pour the sauce over the beef. Serve at once, sprinkled with chopped dill, if liked.

**NOTE:** Creamed or roast parsnips go well with the beef. Malgosia mentioned that, in Poland, she always prepared parsnip tops as well as the roots. I chopped some tender young leaves and found their flavour radish-like, excellent sprinkled over the sauce. A successful mixture of ideas to inspire you to experiment!

## MEATLOAF

A very simple meat roll to serve with boiled potatoes and red cabbage with onion and apple (page 53). Serves 6.

| |
|---|
| *1 dried mushroom or 1 tbsp mushroom ketchup* |
| *1½ lb/675 g/1½ lb minced veal (ground veal)* |
| *1 cup/40 g/1½ oz fresh breadcrumbs* |
| *2 tbsp chopped fresh parsley* |
| *2 tbsp chopped fresh dill (optional)* |
| *salt and freshly ground black pepper* |
| *1 egg, beaten* |
| *a little oil to brush* |

Simmer the dried mushroom, if used, in just enough water to cover for 5 minutes. Drain and chop. Boil the cooking liquid until reduced to 1 tbsp.

Mix the mushroom and cooking liquid or ketchup with all the remaining ingredients, pounding the meat mixture until smooth. All the ingredients should be thoroughly combined. Grease a roasting tin.

Set the oven at 180°C/350°F/gas 4. Shape the meat mixture into a 20 cm/8 in long roll. Place it in the roasting tin and brush all over with oil. Bake for 1 hour, until lightly browned all over, firm and cooked through. Cut into slices to serve.

**NOTE:** One long kabanos (Polish sausage) may be placed in the middle of the roll. Shape the meat into a large flat oblong, put the kabanos down the middle, then press the meat around it.

MEATLOAF

## F ROLLS

Small fingers of bacon fat should be used instead of the bacon in these rolls if possible. If you have a good continental delicatessen near you, buy speck – cured pork fat coated in paprika. Serves 4.

*1 lb/500 g/1 lb frying steak, such as rump*

*1 pickled cucumber (dill pickle), quartered lengthways*

*4 fingers of bacon fat or 2 rashers (slices) rindless bacon, halved*

*4 tbsp plain flour (all purpose flour)*

*salt and freshly ground black pepper*

*a little fat*

*1 small onion, finely chopped*

*2½ cups/600 ml/1 pt water*

*1 bay leaf*

*1 dried mushroom or 6 open mushrooms, sliced*

*⅔ cup/150 ml/¼ pt soured cream*

*2 tbsp chopped fresh parsley*

Cut the steak into four equal pieces. Place each piece in turn between sheets of greaseproof (waxed) paper and beat out until very thin. Use a meat mallet or rolling pin for this. Place a piece of pickled cucumber (dill pickle) and a finger of fat or half bacon rasher (slice) on each slice of steak. Roll up and secure with two wooden cocktail sticks (toothpicks). Coat the rolls with flour and plenty of seasoning.

Heat a little fat in a flameproof casserole – beef dripping is best, butter or oil will do. Add the beef rolls and brown them all over. Add the onion and reduce the heat, then continue to cook for about 5 minutes, stirring the onion as best you can until it is slightly softened. Pour in the water, add the bay leaf and mushroom.

Heat until the liquid is simmering, then cook, uncovered, at a steady simmer for 40 minutes. Turn the rolls over halfway through cooking and baste them often with the liquid. By the time the beef rolls are cooked through the sauce should be reduced by half. Transfer the rolls to a warmed serving dish, remove the cocktail sticks and keep hot.

If there is a lot of liquid in the pan, boil it hard for a few minutes to reduce it to about 1¼ cups/300 ml/½ pt. Achieving the exact quantity is not important but the sauce should be slightly thickened and full flavoured. Remove from the heat and stir in the soured cream. Taste and adjust the seasoning, then warm through without boiling. Stir in the parsley and pour the sauce over the rolls. Serve at once, with boiled potatoes and other vegetables or with łasanki with cabbage (page 67) or buckwheat (page 66).

BEEF ROLLS

## MEATBALLS WITH FRESH TOMATO SAUCE

These meatballs may be served with a variety of sauces – try the mushroom sauce from fried fish with mushroom sauce (page 33) or horseradish sauce from boiled beef with horseradish sauce (page 37). Serve noodles or łazanki with cabbage (page 67) as an accompaniment. Serves 4.

*1 lb/500 g/1 lb minced veal (ground veal)*

*¾ cup/25 g/1 oz fresh white breadcrumbs*

*1 egg, beaten*

*1 tsp dried marjoram*

*salt and freshly ground black pepper*

*2½ cups/600 ml/1 pt veal or chicken stock (page 27)*

### TOMATO SAUCE

*1 onion, chopped*

*2 tbsp/25 g/1 oz butter*

*1 bay leaf*

*2 lb/1 kg/2 lb tomatoes, roughly chopped*

*large parsley sprig*

*1 tsp sugar*

*1 tsp cider vinegar*

*⅔ cup/150 ml/¼ pt soured cream*

Mix the veal, breadcrumbs, egg, marjoram and seasoning, then pound them together until thoroughly combined. Wet your hands and shape the mixture into 16 meatballs about the size of large plums. Make sure they are all nicely smooth.

Heat the stock in a saucepan until just simmering. Add the meatballs, cover and simmer for 25 minutes. Drain the meatballs, reserving the stock. Set aside, covered, while making the sauce.

For the sauce, cook the onion in the butter with the bay leaf in a pan for 10 minutes, until soft. Add the tomatoes, parsley and reserved stock. Bring to the boil, reduce the heat and simmer steadily, uncovered, for 1 hour. Press the sauce through a sieve and return it to the rinsed pan. Add the sugar and vinegar, seasoning to taste and bring to the boil. Add the meatballs and simmer for 10 minutes, or until heated through. Stir in the soured cream, heat very gently without boiling for about 1 minute. Serve at once.

## POLISH SCHNITZEL

Małgosia explained how to make Polish schnitzel. When I tried them they reminded me of the tasty rissoles I used to help my mother make when I was a child. Serves 4.

---

1 onion, very finely chopped

---

2 tbsp / 25 g / 1 oz fat

---

1 cup / 225 g / 8 oz cooked meat, minced (ground)

---

¾ cup / 25 g / 1 oz fresh breadcrumbs

---

salt and freshly ground black pepper

---

2 tbsp chopped fresh parsley

---

1 egg, beaten

---

### COATING

a little flour

---

1 small egg, beaten

---

¾ cup / 50 g / 2 oz fine dry white breadcrumbs

---

oil or fat to cook

---

Cook the onion in the fat for 10 minutes over low heat, or slightly longer, until very soft but not browned. Meat dripping gives the best flavour. Mix the onion with the meat, breadcrumbs, seasoning, parsley and egg, stirring until the mixture is thoroughly bound. Divide into four.

Mould each portion of meat into a thin, flat, oval patty measuring about 13 cm / 5 in long. Coat each schnitzel with a little flour, then brush with beaten egg. Coat with fine crumbs, pressing them on well. Cook the schnitzel in hot oil or fat until golden on both sides. Drain on absorbent kitchen paper and serve at once.

POLISH SCHNITZEL

## VEAL STEW

A familiar Eastern European dish, serve the stew with fresh vegetables, sauerkraut with mushrooms (page 54) or try the cabbage pudding (page 51) for a combination that is not necessarily authentic but very satisfying. Serves 4–6.

---

2 lb / 1 kg / 2 lb stewing veal, cubed

---

2 tbsp / 25 g / 1 oz fat

---

1 clove garlic

---

1 large onion, sliced

---

½ tsp dried marjoram

---

½ tsp ground allspice

---

½ tsp paprika

---

salt and freshly ground black pepper

---

2 tbsp plain flour (all purpose flour)

---

2½ cups / 600 ml / 1 pt veal or chicken stock (page 27) or half and half stock and red wine

---

1 bay leaf

---

2 parsley sprigs

---

1½ lb / 675 g / 1½ lb potatoes, cubed

---

⅔ cup / 150 ml / ¼ pt soured cream

---

Lightly brown the veal in the fat in a heavy-based flameproof casserole. Beef or pork dripping or butter may be used; if you prefer, substitute a little oil. Stir in the garlic and onion and continue to cook until the onion is slightly softened. Stir in the spices, seasoning and flour. Cook for 1 minute, then stir in the stock. Add the bay leaf and parsley (tie them together if you like). Bring to the boil, then reduce the heat so that the stew simmers. Cover and cook for 1 hour, stirring occasionally.

Add the potatoes, stir and cook for a further 20–30 minutes, or until the potatoes are very tender. Lastly stir in the soured cream and heat through for a few minutes. Check the seasoning before serving.

VEAL STEW

## ROAST PORK

Caraway seeds and garlic make this an aromatic roast. Serves 8.

---

*3 lb / 1.5 kg / 3 lb rolled leg of pork (rolled fresh ham)*

*1 large clove garlic*

*salt and freshly ground black pepper*

*2 tsp caraway seeds*

*8 medium cooking apples, peeled, cored and halved*

*5 cups / 1.15 L / 2 pt water*

*2 tbsp honey*

---

Set the oven at 190°C/375°F/gas 5. Make sure the pork rind is well scored, then rub the joint all over with the cut clove of garlic. Place the garlic in a roasting tin. Rub salt all over the rind, then sprinkle the joint with pepper and place it on top of the garlic in the tin.

Roast the joint for 30 minutes. Baste it with the cooking fat and place the apples in the tin around the joint, basting them well. Roast for a further 15 minutes, then transfer the apples to an ovenproof dish, basting them with just a little fat. Set aside. Pour about a third of the water around the pork and continue to roast for about 1½ hours, adding more water from time to time to prevent the base of the pan from drying out.

Trickle the honey over the apples and put them back in the oven for about 10 minutes before serving the joint. Transfer the meat to a warmed serving platter. Boil the cooking liquid (add the extra water if necessary), scraping all the residue from the sides of the roasting tin. When the liquid is reduced to a full-flavoured thin gravy, carve the pork into slices, moisten with a little gravy and serve with the apples.

**NOTE:** For a different size joint, calculate the cooking time at about 30–35 minutes per 450 g/1 lb, plus an extra 30 minutes.

## PORK WITH BEANS

One of my favourite, easy and hearty winter meals, guaranteed to bring a glow to the face after a walk in even the worst of winter weather. Serves 4.

*2 rashers (slices) rindless smoked bacon, diced*

*1 clove garlic, crushed*

*1 leek, sliced*

*1 onion, thinly sliced*

*2 carrots, sliced ·*

*1 bay leaf*

*1 lb/500 g/1 lb lean, boneless pork, cubed*

*1 cup/225 g/8 oz dried butter beans (dried fava or lima beans) beans, soaked overnight*

*salt and freshly ground black pepper*

*5 cups/1.5 L/2 pt water*

*salt and freshly ground black pepper*

*1 lb/500 g/1 lb celeriac, diced*

*2 tbsp plain flour (all purpose flour)*

*4 tbsp soured cream*

*3 tbsp chopped fresh dill or 1 tsp dried dill*

Cook the bacon and garlic in a large, heavy-based flameproof casserole until the fat runs. Add the leek, onion, carrots and bay leaf and cook for about 5 minutes, until the onion begins to soften. Stir in the pork and drained beans. Pour in the water and bring to the boil. Make sure that the beans are well covered with water, adding extra if necessary. Reduce the heat, cover and simmer for 30 minutes. Check to make sure that the beans do not dry up on the surface during cooking.

Add plenty of seasoning at this stage and stir in the celeriac. Continue to cook the stew, half uncovered so that excess liquid evaporates, for a further 30 minutes, or until the beans are cooked.

Stir the flour and soured cream into a smooth paste and add a little cooking liquid from the pot. Stir the paste into the stew and bring to the boil. Simmer for 3 minutes, add the dill and serve.

PORK WITH BEANS

## DUCK WITH RED CABBAGE

Succulent duck portions braised on a bed of red cabbage and apple. Serves 4.

*4–4½ lb/1.75–2 kg/4–4½ lb duck*

*1 small whole onion*

*a little fat*

*1 onion, thinly sliced*

*1 bay leaf*

*½ tsp caraway seeds*

*salt and freshly ground black pepper*

*1 lb/500 g/1 lb red cabbage, shredded*

*1 lb/500 g/1 lb cooking apples, peeled, cored and sliced*

*2 tbsp sugar*

*1 tbsp plain flour (all purpose flour)*

*⅔ cup/150 ml/¼ pt soured cream (optional)*

Trim any large pieces of fat from the duck and trim off the large flap of skin from the neck end. Cut off the ends of the joints and put them in a saucepan. Turn the duck breast down on a board and use a heavy knife to split it along the back. Open out the duck and cut it in half through the inside of the breast. Cut each half into two portions. Trim off the small and broken bones from the breast portion. Add all the trimmings, except lumps of fat, to the joint ends. Wash and dry the duck joints.

Cut the whole onion in half without peeling and add it to the duck trimmings in the saucepan. Pour in water to cover, bring to the boil and simmer, covered, for 40 minutes. Drain the liquid off, return it to the pan and boil it until reduced to 1½ cups/350 ml/12 fl oz.

Meanwhile, brown the duck joints all over in the minimum of fat in a heavy-based flameproof casserole. Drain off excess fat. Add the sliced onion, bay leaf and caraway seeds with plenty of seasoning. Pour in the reduced stock and bring to the boil. Cover and simmer for 30 minutes. Lift the duck joints from the stock. Add the cabbage, apple and sugar, stir well to mix thoroughly, then replace the duck on top. Cover and simmer duck, fruit and vegetable for a further 30 minutes.

Taste and adjust the seasoning. Blend the flour to a smooth paste with the minimum of water, then stir it into the cabbage mixture. Bring to the boil, all the while stirring as best you can. Simmer for 3 minutes and serve. Soured cream may be served with the casserole, if liked.

DUCK WITH RED CABBAGE

## DUCK IN SPICY SAUCE

Serve potatoes or noodles and seasonal vegetables with this lightly spiced duck casserole. Serves 4.

*4 duck portions or joint 1 duck as in duck with red cabbage (page 44)*

*2½ cups/600 ml/1 pt water*

*1 tbsp vinegar*

*a little fat*

*1 onion, chopped*

*1 bay leaf*

*1 tsp ground ginger*

*1 tsp grated nutmeg*

*salt and freshly ground black pepper*

*3¾ cups/900 ml/1/1½ pt chicken stock (page 27) (or stock made from trimmings when jointing duck)*

*1 tbsp plain flour (all purpose flour)*

*4 tbsp soured cream*

Wash the duck joints, then pat dry on absorbent kitchen paper. Put the joints in a bowl, pour the water over them and add the vinegar. Cover and chill overnight.

Drain and dry the duck portions. Cook them in the minimum of fat in a heavy-based flameproof casserole until well browned all over. Drain off excess fat. Add the onion, bay leaf and spices with some seasoning, then pour in the stock. Bring just to the boil, cover and simmer for 45 minutes, until the duck is cooked through and tender. Transfer the duck to a warmed serving dish or plates.

Blend the flour to a smooth paste with the soured cream. Add a little of the stock from the casserole, then pour the mixture into the casserole and bring to the boil, stirring. Simmer for 2 minutes, then pour the sauce over the duck.

WALKING THE COWS HOME

## TRIPE À LA WARSAW

Tripe features often in Polish cookery and I noticed it on the menu at the Polish centre I visited in London. Not being over-familiar with cooking methods for tripe, I have based this recipe on one in Zofia Czerny's Polish Cookbook. Tripe sold in supermarkets is usually ready-washed and boiled until tender. Serves 4.

*1 lb/500 g tripe*

*salt and freshly ground black pepper*

*2 bay leaves*

*¼ cup/50 g/2 oz butter*

*1 onion, chopped*

*1 leek, sliced*

*1 carrot, sliced*

*1 parsnip, cubed*

*2 celery sticks, sliced*

*½ tsp ground allspice*

*½ tsp ground ginger*

*¼ tsp grated nutmeg*

*½ tsp dried marjoram*

*¼ cup/25 g/1 oz plain flour (all purpose flour)*

*2½ cups/600 ml/1 pt good beef stock*

*1⅓ cups/50 g/2 oz fresh breadcrumbs*

*2 tbsp chopped fresh parsley*

*2 tbsp grated Parmesan cheese*

*2 eggs, hard-boiled (hard-cooked) and chopped*

*a handful of small parsley sprigs*

Thoroughly wash the tripe under cold running water and scrape it all over with a kitchen knife. Be sure to thoroughly scrape and wash all the honeycomb sections. Wash again before plunging the tripe into a saucepan of simmering water. Bring to a full boil, boil for 5 minutes, then drain and rinse the tripe well. Squeeze all the water out of the tripe. Place it in the rinsed pan and pour in water to cover. Add some salt and the bay leaves. Bring to the boil, cover and cook for about 4 hours, or until the tripe is tender. Top up with fresh boiling water as necessary to keep the tripe covered. Drain, rinse and squeeze out the cooked tripe. Cut it into short, fine strips and set aside.

Melt half the butter in a large saucepan and add all the vegetables. Cook, stirring occasionally, for about 20 minutes, or until the onion is tender. Stir in the spices, marjoram and flour with some seasoning. Stirring all the time, gradually pour in the stock and bring to the boil. Reduce the heat and simmer for 20 minutes, until the vegetables are tender. Meanwhile, set the oven at 190°C/375°F/gas 5.

Stir the tripe into the sauce, then pour the mixture into an ovenproof dish. Melt the remaining butter in a small pan. Stir in the breadcrumbs and cook for 2 minutes, then remove from the heat and add the parsley. Stir in the cheese with a little pepper and sprinkle this mixture all over the tripe.

Bake for 20 minutes, until golden on top. Arrange the chopped egg in two lines across the top of the crumbs, adding a neat garnish of parsley sprigs all the way along. Serve at once with buttered potatoes.

## ROAST TURKEY

Roast turkey is uncomplicated and familiar; the stuffing is pleasingly different. Turkey used to be very popular and prized for its quality in centuries past. It would have been eaten on Christmas day, although most households would also eat up the remains of puddings and sweet delights from the Christmas eve meal.

This recipe serves 8–10.

| |
|---|
| 8 lb/3.5 kg/8 lb turkey with giblets |
| 1 small onion, quartered |
| 1 bay leaf |
| 1 large onion, finely chopped |
| 1/4 cup/50 g/2 oz butter |
| salt and freshly ground black pepper |
| 1/2 tsp ground ginger |
| 1/2 tsp grated nutmeg |
| 1/2 tsp ground allspice |
| good pinch of ground cloves |
| 2/3 cup/100 g/4 oz raisins |
| 3 tbsp chopped fresh parsley |
| 5 1/3 cups/225 g/8 oz fresh breadcrumbs |
| 2 eggs, separated |
| 3 tbsp plain flour (all purpose flour) |

Trim the wing ends off the turkey. Cut away any lumps of fat and singe off any small feathers with a long match – let the match burn for just a few seconds before doing this to avoid making the turkey smokey. Rinse the bird inside and out under cold running water, then dry it thoroughly with absorbent kitchen paper.

Chop the turkey liver and set aside. Put the other giblets in a pan with the wing ends, quartered onion and bay leaf. Pour on water to cover, bring to the boil, cover and simmer for 1 hour. Strain this stock for making gravy.

Cook the onion in half the butter for about 15 minutes, or until softened but not browned. Stir in the chopped turkey liver and cook until firm. Add seasoning, all the spices and the raisins. Continue to cook, stirring all the time, for 2–3 minutes, until the raisins are slightly plump. Add the parsley, then pour the cooked mixture over the breadcrumbs and mix well. Mix in the egg yolks until they are evenly distributed. Whisk the egg whites until they stand in soft peaks and stir them into the stuffing.

Set the oven at 180°C/350°F/gas 4. Spoon the stuffing into the neck end of the bird and put the rest into the body cavity. Truss the turkey neatly with string, tying the wings together, then bringing the string up to the legs and tie it off. Smear the remaining butter over the turkey breast. Roast, covered with foil, for 2 1/2 hours. Baste the bird frequently with the cooking juices.

Pour off most of the fat from the roasting tin and add some of the giblet stock, stirring the roasting residue off the sides of the tin around the turkey. Roast the bird, covered, for a further 15 minutes. Uncover and continue to cook for 30–45 minutes, until the turkey is browned and cooked through. Pierce the bird at the thickest part of the thigh to see if the meat is cooked: if there is any sign of pink meat or blood then continue to roast the turkey.

Keep topping up the stock in the roasting tin to make a rich gravy. When the turkey is cooked, strain the cooking juices. Thicken them with the flour blended with a little water. Bring to the boil and simmer for 3 minutes.

## ROAST CHICKEN WITH BUCKWHEAT

If you would prefer to stuff the chicken with a breadcrumb mixture, try the dill stuffing described in the note at the end of the recipe. Serves 4–6.

---

*1 cup/175 g/6 oz roasted buckwheat*

*2 cups/475 ml/16 fl oz water*

*1 onion, finely chopped*

*2 tbsp/25 g/1 oz butter*

*1 clove garlic, crushed (optional)*

*¼ lb/100 g/4 oz chicken livers, chopped*

*½ tsp dried marjoram*

*salt and freshly ground black pepper*

*1 egg, beaten*

*3½ lb/1.5 kg/3½ lb oven-ready chicken*

---

Place the buckwheat in a sieve and rinse under cold running water. Put the buckwheat in a saucepan and pour in the water. Heat very gently until the water is just about simmering. Remove the pan from the heat, cover and leave for 30 minutes by which time the buckwheat should have absorbed all the water.

Cook the onion in the butter for 10 minutes, until soft but not browned. Add the garlic and chicken livers and cook for a further 5 minutes, stirring occasionally, until the pieces of liver are firm. Add this mixture to the buckwheat with the marjoram and seasoning to taste. Stir in the egg to bind, making sure all the ingredients are thoroughly combined.

Set the oven at 180°C/350°F/gas 4. Rinse the chicken under cold running water, drain well and pat dry with absorbent kitchen paper. Spoon the stuffing into the body cavity and truss the bird neatly, tying string around the legs and wings. Place in a roasting tin. Roast for 1¾ hours, or until the chicken is golden, crisp and cooked through. Halfway through cooking, pour a little water into the bottom of the roasting tin and keep topping this up as it evaporates.

Transfer the cooked chicken to a warmed serving plate. Add a little extra water to the cooking juices, if necessary, and boil the liquid, scraping all the roasting residue off the pan. When the gravy is reduced and flavoursome, check the seasoning and serve a little poured over the chicken.

**NOTE:** To make a dill stuffing, cook 1 small onion in 2 tbsp/25 g/1 oz butter until soft. Mix the onion with 4 cups/175 g/6 oz fresh white breadcrumbs, 4 tbsp chopped fresh dill, salt and freshly ground black pepper and 2 egg yolks. Whisk the whites until they peak softly, then stir into the stuffing.

## ROAST VENISON WITH JUNIPER

Venison is increasingly popular and more readily available in supermarkets as well as good butchers. This is a simple method of cooking a roasting joint, based on an old fashioned Polish method from days when venison was freely available. Offer boiled potatoes and cauliflower topped with browned, buttered breadcrumbs with the venison. Beetroot (beet) in soured cream sauce (page 57) may also be served as an accompaniment. This recipe serves 8.

| |
|---|
| 3 lb/1.5 kg/3 lb rolled haunch of venison |
| 2½ cups/600 ml/1 pt water |
| 1 onion, sliced |
| 3 bay leaves |
| 3 tbsp vinegar |
| ¼ lb/100 g/4 oz bacon fat |
| 1 parsnip, diced |
| 1 carrot, diced |
| 1 leek, sliced |
| ¼ lb/100 g/4 oz celeriac, diced |
| 4 juniper berries |
| 4 allspice berries |
| salt and freshly ground black pepper |
| ¼ cup/50 g/2 oz rendered bacon or pork fat or butter |
| 1¼ cups/300 ml/½ pt red wine |
| 1¼ cups/300 ml/½ pt soured cream |

Make sure that the venison is trimmed of all fat and membranes, as venison fat has an unpleasant taste. Put the joint of venison in a bowl. Heat the water, onion and 2 bay leaves slowly until boiling. Reduce the heat, cover and simmer for 5 minutes. Allow to cool completely, then add the vinegar and pour the mixture over the venison. Cover and chill for 24 hours, turning the joint at least twice.

Cut the bacon fat into strips. Drain the venison and pat it dry on absorbent kitchen paper. Use a meat skewer to pierce holes through the joint. Use a larding needle to thread the bacon fat through the holes. If you do not have a larding needle, then use the meat skewer to push the fat into the joint as far as possible. This is known as 'larding', a process of introducing fat to very lean meat to keep it moist during cooking.

ROAST VENISON WITH JUNIPER

Set the oven at 190°C/375°'F/gas 5. Place all the vegetables in a roasting tin with the remaining bay leaf. Crush the juniper and allspice and mix with seasoning, then rub the mixture all over the venison. Stand the joint on the vegetables and smear it generously with fat or butter. Roast the venison for 1 hour, basting often with fat, adding extra fat if necessary, to keep the meat moist. The venison should be cooked until still slightly pink in the middle.

Transfer the joint to a serving platter and keep hot. Pour the wine over the vegetables in the pan and heat slowly, stirring all the time until boiling. Simmer for 5 minutes, stirring and scraping the pan all the time. Sieve the sauce, stir in the soured cream and taste for seasoning. Heat gently, then serve the sauce with the venison, carved into thick slices.

# 5

# VEGETABLES

Vegetables are an important food in Polish cooking. They are used in a great many ways to bulk out meals. Root vegetables are particularly common and the leaves are often eaten, for example with beetroot (beet) in soup, or parsnip leaves may be chopped up and cooked as well as being sprinkled over cooked food or salad as a tasty garnish.

Cabbage and sauerkraut feature in a great many dishes: served simply with soured cream or a thickened sauce, or united to flavour bigos (page 36). Either may be used as a filling for dumplings or pancakes, and cabbage makes a surprisingly delicious filling for cabbage and mushroom rolls (page 18). Zofia Czerny includes a number of vegetable puddings in Polish Cooking, so I experimented with a cabbage pudding and found that it made a delicious supper dish.

Salads are just as popular as hot dishes, notably a fiery concoction of grated beetroot with horseradish which is delicious with boiled beef. Cucumber is served with soured cream, red cabbage is briefly salted to make a salad and tomatoes may be served topped with chopped onion. In Poland, celery root is an essential vegetable for flavouring stews; celeriac acts only as a reasonable substitute. Beans, fresh and dried, particularly dried white beans are added to soups and stews. They may also be served cold in salad. Małgosia told me of a dish combining cooked butter beans (dried fava or lima beans) with garlic and tomatoes.

This chapter offers a sample of Polish vegetable cookery, providing suggestions for side dishes and some delicious snacks. Plain, boiled seasonal vegetables, dressed with melted butter or buttery, lightly fried breadcrumbs are a classic accompaniment.

CABBAGE PUDDING

## CABBAGE PUDDING

Serve a mushroom sauce (page 33) or horseradish sauce (page 32) with this pudding. Alternatively, mix 2–3 tbsp grated horseradish into ⅔ cup/150 ml/ ¼ pt soured cream to make a refreshing accompaniment. Serves 4–6.

---

*1 leek, chopped*

*2 tbsp/25 g/1 oz fat*

*1½ lb/675 g/1½ lb green cabbage, trimmed of tough stalk*

*1⅓ cups/50 g/2 oz fresh breadcrumbs*

*salt and freshly ground black pepper*

*a little grated nutmeg*

*3 tbsp soured cream*

*3 eggs*

***TOPPING***

*¼ cup/50 g/2 oz butter*

*1 cup/40 g/1½ oz fresh breadcrumbs*

*2 tbsp chopped fresh dill*

*1 egg, hard-boiled (hard-cooked) and chopped*

---

Cook the leek in the fat for about 5 minutes, until soft. Boil the cabbage for 5 minutes. Drain well and cool, then squeeze out all the water.

Finely chop the cabbage by hand or in a food processor. Mix the cabbage with the leek, breadcrumbs, plenty of seasoning and some grated nutmeg. It is a good idea to taste the mixture at this stage for flavour – the seasoning must be complementary but not too strong. If you use too much nutmeg it will dominate the pudding when it is steamed. Mix in the soured cream and eggs.

Line the base of an 18 cm/7 in soufflé dish with greaseproof (waxed) paper and grease the inside of the dish well. Spoon the cabbage mixture into the dish, pressing it down evenly with the back of a spoon. Cover with buttered greaseproof paper and a double thick piece of foil. Crumple the foil edges securely around the rim of the dish or tie securely to exclude all steam.

Steam the pudding over rapidly boiling water for 40 minutes, topping up the water if necessary. The pudding should feel firm and light.

Prepare the topping just before the pudding is cooked: melt the butter and cook the breadcrumbs until golden. Stir in the dill and egg. Slide a knife around between the pudding and dish, then turn out on to a warmed serving plate. Spoon the topping over the pudding. Serve at once.

STUFFED CABBAGE LEAVES

## CABBAGE WITH KABANOS

Not terribly traditional but delicious for supper with chunks of Polish rye bread (page 72). A small amount of diced smoked pork or smoked bacon would be a more authentic flavouring for the cabbage in place of kabanos. Serves 4.

*1 large onion, thinly sliced*

*2 tbsp / 25 g / 1 oz fat*

*½ lb / 225 g / 8 oz kabanos, sliced*

*1½ lb / 675 g / 1½ lb green cabbage, trimmed of tough stalk and shredded*

*1¼ cups / 300 ml / ½ pt water*

*salt and freshly ground black pepper*

*1 tbsp plain flour (all purpose flour)*

*4 tbsp soured cream*

In a heavy-based flameproof casserole, cook the onion in the fat for about 15 minutes, until soft but not browned. Add the kabanos, stir well and cook for 2 minutes. Stir in the cabbage, then pour in the water and add a little seasoning. Bring to the boil, cover and cook, just boiling, for 5 minutes.

Stir the flour with the soured cream to make a smooth paste. Stir the paste into the cabbage and simmer, stirring all the time, for a further 3–5 minutes, until thick and the cabbage is well cooked. Taste for seasoning before serving.

## RED CABBAGE WITH ONION AND APPLE

Another of the famous dishes of Eastern Europe, this method of cooking red cabbage results in a tempting combination of sweet and sour. It is perfect with all sorts of pork, particularly grilled (broiled) chops, and excellent with boiled smoked Polish sausage (wiejska). White cabbage may be used in place of red. Serves 4.

---

1 large onion, thinly sliced

2 tsp caraway seeds

2 tbsp/25 g/1 oz fat

1¼ lb/575 g/1¼ lb red cabbage, shredded

½ cup/100 ml/4 fl oz water

2 tbsp sugar

salt and freshly ground black pepper

1 large cooking apple, peeled, cored and diced

1 tbsp vinegar

---

In a heavy-based flameproof casserole, cook the onion and caraway seeds in the fat for about 15 minutes, until soft but not browned. Stir frequently and keep the heat fairly low to prevent the onion from browning. Stir in the cabbage, pour in the water, then add the sugar and seasoning. Heat until simmering, cover and cook for 30 minutes.

Stir in the apple and vinegar. Cook, uncovered, for about 20 minutes so that the excess water evaporates. Stir frequently to prevent the cabbage sticking to the pot. Taste for seasoning before serving.

## STUFFED CABBAGE LEAVES

Known as gołabki, these may be filled with meat (pork or lamb), rice, a combination of both or with buckwheat.

Eva told me that gołabki literally means pigeon, and recalled her horror as a very small child at the thought of eating the pigeons flying about outside when her mother announced that she had cooked gołabki for dinner.

Gołabki may be made using very large cabbage leaves, serving just one per portion with a little unthickened cooking liquid poured over. Alternatively, they may be dressed with a tomato or béchamel-type sauce. Here I have thickened the cooking juices and added soured cream to make a delicious sauce. Serves 4.

---

8 large green cabbage leaves

1 onion, finely chopped

2 tbsp/25 g/1 oz butter

½ cup/100 g/4 oz cooked pork or lamb, diced

½ cup/100 g/4 oz long-grain rice, cooked and cooled

1 cup/100 g/4 oz mushrooms, chopped (use chestnut mushrooms for a good flavour)

½ tsp dried marjoram

2 tbsp chopped fresh parsley

salt and freshly ground black pepper

1 cup/250 ml/8 fl oz stock, such as chicken or beef (page 27)

2 tbsp plain flour (all purpose flour)

2 tbsp water

⅔ cup/150 ml/¼ pt soured cream

---

Cook the cabbage in boiling water for 2–3 minutes, until pliable. Drain well, dry on absorbent kitchen paper and trim away a small 'V' shape from any hard stalks.

Cook the onion in the butter for 10 minutes, until soft. Stir in the meat, rice, mushrooms, herbs and seasoning. Mix well and cook for 1 minute. Roughly divide this filling into eight.

Place a portion of filling on each leaf, slightly nearer the stalk end than in the middle. Fold the stalk end over the filling, then fold the sides of the leaf over. Roll the stuffing and leaf from the stalk end to make a neat parcel. Put into a medium saucepan, join down. Stuff the other leaves and pack them fairly tightly into the pan. If the pan is too large to hold the leaves, use a smaller one. Pour in the stock and heat until simmering. Cover and cook for 20 minutes.

Transfer the gołabki to a warmed serving dish. Blend the flour with the water and stir into the cooking liquid. Bring to the boil, stirring, then add the soured cream and stir until hot. Taste for seasoning, pour this sauce over the gołabki and serve.

SAUERKRAUT WITH MUSHROOMS

## SAUERKRAUT WITH MUSHROOMS

Dried mushrooms enrich sauerkraut but the vegetable may be cooked with a sauce made from meat stock instead. Offer as a side dish to grilled (broiled) or roast pork, boiled beef or other meats, including roast game. Serves 2–4.

*2 large dried mushrooms*

*1¼ cups/300 ml/½ pt water*

*1 onion, thinly sliced*

*2 tbsp/25 g/1 oz butter*

*1 tbsp plain flour (all purpose flour)*

*1 lb/500 g/1 lb sauerkraut, drained*

*⅔ cup/150 ml/¼ pt soured cream*

*salt and freshly ground black pepper*

Simmer the mushrooms in the water for 5 minutes. Drain, reserving the liquor, and chop the mushrooms. Cook the onion in the butter for 10 minutes, until softened but not browned. Stir in the flour, then gradually add the mushroom liquor and bring to the boil. Add the mushrooms to the sauce.

Squeeze the sauerkraut to extract all the liquid (save some to add at the end of cooking if you like fairly sour vegetables), then slice the pat of vegetable with a sharp knife to shred it. Add to the sauce, stirring well. Cover and simmer for 20 minutes.

Stir in the soured cream, heat gently and taste for seasoning before serving.

## RED CABBAGE SALAD

A simple crunchy salad to serve with boiled beef, fried meat or with cold meat and fish such as herrings. I like a crunchy salad as an accompaniment to dumplings, such as kopytka (page 62), pierogi (page 64) or leniwe pierogi (page 61). Serves 4.

*½ lb/225 g/8 oz red cabbage, trimmed of tough stalk, and shredded*

*salt and freshly ground black pepper*

*1 small onion or ½ large onion, very finely sliced*

*4 tart eating apples, peeled, cored and coarsely grated*

*1 tbsp cider vinegar*

*1 tbsp sugar*

*2 tbsp olive oil*

*2 tsp Dijon or mild German mustard*

Place the cabbage in a colander, sprinkling each layer with a little salt. Leave to drain over a bowl for 2–3 hours. Shake all the moisture from the cabbage, then pat it on absorbent kitchen paper. Toss the cabbage with the onion and apples.

Mix the vinegar and sugar until the sugar has dissolved. Whisk in the oil and mustard, adding a little pepper. Toss this dressing into the salad and serve.

**NOTE:** A little natural yogurt or soured cream is delicious trickled over the salad with a little chopped fresh dill – but this is a departure from authenticity!

RED CABBAGE SALAD

POTATO PANCAKES

## POTATO PANCAKES

These pancakes are delicious and they freeze well, so why not make a large batch and freeze some for another day? As a child Eva would eat potato pancakes as a snack, dredged with sugar; although they are occasionally eaten with sugar, they are served mainly as a savoury dish. Add grated onion and/or crushed garlic to the mixture if you like. Makes 8.

*1½ lb/675 g/1½ lb potatoes, peeled and grated*

*¼ cup/25 g/1 oz plain flour (all purpose flour)*

*salt and freshly ground black pepper*

*1 egg, beaten*

*oil or fat to cook*

Rinse and drain the potatoes, squeezing all the water from them. Mix the flour, plenty of seasoning and the egg with the potatoes, stirring well to make sure the ingredients are thoroughly combined.

Heat a little fat or oil in a large frying pan (skillet). Drop spoonfuls of the mixture into the hot fat, spreading it out evenly and thinly, making the edges as neat as possible. Cook over a medium heat for about 4 minutes on each side, until the pancakes are golden and crisp outside, tender through the middle. Drain on absorbent kitchen paper and serve at once.

CARROT AND POTATO HOTPOT

# CARROT AND POTATO HOTPOT

A simple, warming vegetable dish. Serves 4.

*1 large onion, thinly sliced*

*6 tbsp/75 g/3 oz butter*

*¾ lb/350 g/12 oz carrots, thickly sliced*

*1½ lb/675 g/1½ lb potatoes, peeled and cut in large chunks*

*salt and freshly ground black pepper*

*1 bay leaf*

*2½ cups/600 ml/1 pt water*

*⅔ cup/25 g/1 oz fresh breadcrumbs*

*6 tbsp/40 g/1½ oz plain flour (all purpose flour)*

*⅔ cup/150 ml/¼ pt soured cream*

*2 tbsp chopped fresh dill*

Cook the onion in one third of the butter for 10 minutes. Stir in the carrots and potatoes, then sprinkle in some seasoning. Add the bay leaf and pour in the water. Bring to the boil, then simmer, uncovered, for about 15 minutes, until the vegetables are tender.

Meanwhile, cook the breadcrumbs in half the remaining butter until golden. Set aside.

Drain the vegetables, reserving the liquid, and put them in a warmed serving dish. Melt the remaining butter in a saucepan and stir in the flour. Gradually add the cooking liquid and bring to the boil, stirring. Simmer for 3 minutes, add the soured cream and dill, and taste for seasoning. Pour this sauce over the vegetables and top with the crumbs. Serve at once.

## POTATO SALAD

This is delicious with herrings in soured cream (page 14). Serves 4–6.

| |
|---|
| 2 lb/1 kg/2 lb potatoes |
| 2 tsp sugar |
| 2 tbsp cider vinegar |
| salt and freshly ground black pepper |
| 4 tbsp olive oil |
| 4 tbsp snipped chives |
| 2 tbsp chopped fresh dill |
| **GARNISH** |
| 1 small onion, very thinly sliced |
| 2 eggs, hard-boiled (hard-cooked) and sliced |
| dill sprigs |

Boil the potatoes in their skins for about 20 minutes, until tender. Cool the potatoes until you can handle them, then peel. Cut into neat cubes and place in a dish.

Stir the sugar with the vinegar until the sugar has dissolved. Whisk in the seasoning, oil and herbs. Pour this dressing over the potatoes and toss lightly. Garnish with onion, sliced egg and dill just before serving.

POTATO SALAD

BEETROOT IN SOUR CREAM SAUCE

## BEETROOT (BEET) IN SOURED CREAM SAUCE

Sugar and vinegar are added to give the beetroot (beet) a sweet and sour flavour. The vegetable is served with cooked meat, fish, game or poultry. Serves 4.

| |
|---|
| 1 large onion, finely chopped |
| 2 tbsp/25 g/1 oz butter |
| 1 tbsp plain flour (all purpose flour) |
| 1 tbsp sugar |
| 2 tsp cider vinegar |
| 1 tbsp beetroot (beet) juice |
| 2/3 cup/150 ml/1/4 pt soured cream |
| 1 lb/500 g/1 lb freshly cooked beetroot (beet), peeled and coarsely grated |
| salt and freshly ground black pepper |

Cook the onion in the butter for 15 minutes, until very soft but not browned. Stir in the flour, then add the sugar, vinegar, beetroot juice and soured cream.

Bring to the boil, then stir in the beetroot with a little seasoning. Cook, stirring occasionally, for 5 minutes. Check the seasoning and balance of sweet to sour before serving.

## BRAISED CUCUMBER WITH DILL

This is deliciously delicate: good with chicken or fish. Serves 4.

*1 cucumber, peeled and halved lengthways (about 1 lb / 500 g / 1 lb)*

*1 small onion, halved and thinly sliced*

*2 tbsp / 25 g / 1 oz butter*

*salt and freshly ground black pepper*

*⅔ cup / 150 ml / ¼ pt water*

*1 tbsp sugar*

*1 tbsp cider vinegar*

*2 tbsp soured cream*

*2 tbsp chopped fresh dill*

Use a teaspoon to scoop all the seeds out of the cucumber. Cut each half into 5 cm/2 in lengths. Cook the onion in the butter for 10 minutes. Add the cucumber and stir for 2 minutes to coat the pieces. Sprinkle in seasoning, then pour in the water and heat until simmering. Cover and cook for 5 minutes. Remove the lid and cook for a further 5 minutes, so that some of the water evaporates. The cucumber should be tender but not soft.

Stir in the sugar, vinegar and soured cream. Taste the sauce and adjust the seasoning before serving. Sprinkle with dill.

BRAISED CUCUMBER WITH DILL

## BEETROOT (BEET) SALAD WITH HORSERADISH

Neill, my husband, was served this salad as an accompaniment to boiled beef with horseradish sauce at a Polish club in London. The salad was quite hot with horseradish, so for an authentic flavour you could almost double the quantity of horseradish I use below. Serves 4.

*1 lb / 500 g / 1 lb freshly cooked beetroot (beet)*

*⅔ cup / 150 ml / ¼ pt soured cream*

*2–3 tbsp grated horseradish*

*salt and freshly ground black pepper*

Peel and coarsely grate the beetroot into a serving bowl. Mix in the soured cream and horseradish, adding seasoning to taste. Leave to stand for 15–30 minutes before serving.

## PURÉED PEAS

I made this simple vegetable accompaniment using frozen peas and we ate it with boiled Polish sausage – it was delicious. The pea purée may be served with roast, grilled (broiled) or boiled meats, poultry and game, or with fish. Serves 4.

*1 lb / 500 g / 1 lb shelled peas, frozen or fresh*

*1 small onion, finely chopped*

*6 slices / 100 g / 4 oz smoked rindless streaky bacon, diced*

*1 clove garlic, crushed*

*salt and freshly ground black pepper*

*⅔ cup / 150 ml / ¼ pt soured cream*

Cook the peas in boiling water until tender – about 20 minutes. Drain and purée the peas by pressing them through a sieve or blending in a food processor or blender.

Cook the onion and bacon together for about 20 minutes until the fat runs from the bacon and the onion is soft, stirring frequently. Stir in the garlic, pea purée and seasoning, then heat through. Transfer to a warmed serving dish and swirl the soured cream through the purée. Stir the cream into the purée as you are serving it.

POLISH-STYLE CAULIFLOWER

## CUCUMBER SALAD

Cucumber salad may be served with chicken or fish. It would also be offered as an accompaniment to boiled meats. Serves 4.

*½ cucumber, peeled (about ½ lb / 225 g / 8 oz)*

*salt and freshly ground black pepper*

*⅔ cup / 150 ml / ¼ pt soured cream*

*1 tbsp chopped fresh dill*

Thinly slice the cucumber and place the slices in a colander, sprinkling the layers with a little salt. Stand the colander over a bowl and leave to drain for 15 minutes.

Shake all the liquid off the cucumber and pat the slices dry on absorbent kitchen paper. Mix with the soured cream, adding pepper to taste. Sprinkle with dill and serve.

## POLISH-STYLE CAULIFLOWER

When this topping of breadcrumbs, browned in butter, is used the dish may take the title 'à la Polonaise'. Serves 4.

*1 cauliflower, cut into florets*

*salt and freshly ground black pepper*

*¼ cup / 50 g / 2 oz butter*

*1 cup / 40 g / 1½ oz fresh breadcrumbs*

*a little chopped fresh dill (optional)*

Cook the cauliflower in boiling salted water for about 5 minutes, or until tender. Drain thoroughly and transfer to a warmed serving dish.

Melt the butter and add the breadcrumbs. Cook, stirring, until golden. Add a little seasoning and some dill, if liked. Sprinkle this topping over the cauliflower and serve.

**6**

# DUMPLINGS, NOODLES AND GRAINS

Sadly, I put on rather a lot of weight when I tested the recipes in this chapter. When I set about making different types of dumplings I found that they were, without exception, delicious. The filled dumplings are particularly appetizing and the stuffing may be varied to suit individual tastes. Meat, sauerkraut, dried mushrooms and cooked cabbage all make tasty fillings. Some of the plain dumplings and the tiny noodles may be served as side dishes but, on the whole, these recipes would be served as a main dish.

Whatever dough you make, it should hold together and form a neat smooth dumpling before cooking. The doughs vary enormously and some are quite soft, even so they should form an even coating when moulded.

For the larger, softer dumplings have a draining spoon ready, both to lower them into the cooking liquid and for lifting them out when they are ready for serving. The smaller, firmer dumplings made of pasta-like doughs may be drained in a colander.

The cooking time is important when boiling dumplings because some types will disintegrate when overcooked and others will taste soggy. For the dumplings to cook successfully and fairly quickly, make sure that you have a pan large enough to contain the dumplings and plenty of boiling water. The water must not boil too vigorously, neither must it simmer too slowly. If you are unused to cooking dumplings, it is a good idea to boil a sample specimen first – and taste it, of course – to make sure it is cooked and perfectly delicious!

## KNEDLE

Knedle are made from a potato dough. They may be filled with a savoury stuffing or with fruit (page 68). I have included a sauerkraut stuffing and a dried mushroom stuffing; the quantities given are enough to fill the whole batch of dough, so select one type only. Alternatively, you may prefer a cottage cheese filling, minced (ground) cooked meat stuffing or a simple filling of chopped onion cooked in butter. Serves 4 (16 knedle).

---

*1 lb/500 g/1 lb potatoes*

*½ cup/50 g/2 oz plain flour (all purpose flour)*

*5 tbsp/65 g/2½ oz butter, melted*

*salt and freshly ground black pepper*

*1 small egg*

**SAUERKRAUT FILLING**

*1 small onion, finely chopped*

*a little butter*

*¼ lb/100 g/4 oz sauerkraut, drained*

**MUSHROOM FILLING**

*2 dried mushrooms*

*1⅓ cups/50 g/2 oz fresh white breadcrumbs*

*a little butter, melted*

---

Boil the potatoes in their skins until tender – about 20 minutes. Drain, cool, then peel. Rub the potatoes through a sieve. Mix in the flour, 1 tbsp of the melted butter, ½ tsp salt and the egg. Knead the mixture together and cover. Prepare the chosen filling.

For the sauerkraut filling, cook the onion in a little butter until soft – about 10 minutes. Squeeze all liquid from the sauerkraut, then slice the pat of vegetable into shreds. Mix the sauerkraut and onion, adding a little seasoning.

For the mushroom filling, cook the mushrooms in water to cover for 5 minutes. Drain, reserving the cooking liquid, and chop. Boil the cooking liquid until reduced to 2 tbsp. Mix the mushrooms, breadcrumbs, liquid and a little butter with seasoning to taste.

Divide the dough into eight. Flatten a portion in the palm of your hand, then place an eighth of the chosen filling in the middle and fold the dough around it. Work the dough into a ball to enclose the filling in an even, not too thick, covering. Repeat with the remaining dough and filling, dusting your hands with flour occasionally.

Bring a saucepan of water to the boil, then reduce the heat so it boils steadily. Cook the knedle for 2–3 minutes, until firm and cooked. Drain and serve at once, dressed with the remaining melted butter.

## LENIWE PIEROGI

Leniwe translates to mean lazy – presumably these cheese dumplings were traditionally considered to be a quick alternative to making cheese-filled pierogi. Anyway, they are delicious and quite light. They are usually served as a main course, moistened with melted butter or a topping of breadcrumbs browned in butter may be added. Serves 4 (about 40 dumplings).

---

*¾ lb/350 g/12 oz potatoes*

*1 cup/225 g/8 oz cottage cheese*

*½ cup/50 g/2 oz plain flour (all purpose flour)*

*½ tsp salt*

*⅔ cup/25 g/1 oz fine fresh white breadcrumbs*

*1 egg*

*¼ cup/50 g/2 oz butter*

---

Boil the potatoes in their skins until tender – about 20 minutes. Drain, cool, then peel. Rub the potatoes through a fine sieve. Drain any liquid from the cottage cheese, then rub it through a sieve. Add to the potatoes. Mix in the flour, salt, breadcrumbs and egg to make a soft dough.

Lightly knead the dough into a ball and cut it in half. On a floured surface, use your fingers to roll the dough into a long thin sausage. It should be about 1 cm/½ in thick, or just slightly more and about 62.5–75 cm/25–30 in long. Cut the dough diagonally into dumplings measuring about 2.5–3.5 cm/1–1½ in long. Pat the cut ends with your fingers to seal them slightly. Repeat with the remaining dough.

Bring a large saucepan of water to the boil, then reduce the heat so that the water is not boiling too furiously. Cook the dumplings for 2–3 minutes, then drain. Test one dumpling just to check that they are cooked – if these are overcooked they will fall apart. Melt the butter and pour it over the dumplings. Serve at once – delicious!

## KOPYTKA

The unmistakable similarity between these potato dumplings and potato gnocchi reflects the Italian influence on Polish cooking. They may be served as an accompaniment or as a main dish. Serves 4 (about 30 dumplings).

*1 lb / 500 g / 1 lb potatoes*

*1 cup / 100 g / 4 oz plain flour (all purpose flour)*

*½ tsp salt*

*1 egg*

*¼ cup / 50 g / 2 oz butter*

Boil the potatoes in their skins until tender – about 20 minutes. Drain, cool, then peel. Rub the potatoes through a fine sieve. Stir in the flour and salt. Mix in the egg to make a soft dough.

Take small portions of the dough, slightly smaller than walnuts, and roll into smooth balls. Make a deep indentation in each ball using your index finger. Alternatively, the kopytka may be moulded into slightly squarer shapes.

Bring a saucepan of water to the boil, then reduce the heat so that it is bubbling gently. Add the kopytka and keep the water just bubbling. Cook for 4–5 minutes, until the little dumplings are firm and cooked. Taste one to make sure that they do not taste of raw flour. Do not overcook the kopytka or they will become soggy. Drain well and place in a warmed serving dish. Melt the butter and pour it over the dumplings. Serve at once.

USZKA

## USZKA

These small stuffed dumplings are similar to Italian annellini. However, uszka are filled with dried mushroom stuffing and are the classic accompaniment for beetroot (beet) soup. Serves 4–6 (about 49 uszka).

*1 cup / 100 g / 4 oz plain flour (all purpose flour)*

*salt and freshly ground black pepper*

*1 egg*

*1 tbsp water*

*beaten egg to seal*

***FILLING***

*2 dried mushrooms*

*⅔ cup / 25 g / 1 oz fresh breadcrumbs*

*1 small onion, grated*

*2 tbsp / 25 g / 1 oz butter*

Sift the flour into a bowl with ½ tsp salt. Make a well in the middle, then add the egg and water. Mix to form a firm dough and knead with your hands until smooth. Wrap the dough in cling film (plastic wrap) while you prepare the filling.

Simmer the mushrooms in water to cover for 5 minutes, then drain. Boil the cooking liquor until reduced to 2 tbsp and reserve. Chop the mushrooms and mix them with the breadcrumbs. Cook the onion in the butter for 5 minutes, stirring all the time. Add the cooked onion to the mixture with the reduced cooking liquor and seasoning to taste.

On a lightly floured surface, roll out the dough into a 31 cm / 12½ in square. Cut it horizontally into seven strips, then cut vertically to divide each strip into seven squares. Place a little filling on each square and brush the edges of the dough with beaten egg. Fold the squares of dough in half to make triangular dumplings, sealing the edges well to enclose the filling. Wrap the long side of each triangle around the tip of your finger and pinch their corners together.

Cook the uszka in a saucepan of boiling salted water for about 3 minutes, until the dough is cooked and the filling hot. Drain and serve at once with beetroot (beet) soup.

**NOTE:** Although it is not the authentic way of serving them, uszka taste delicious tossed with butter and eaten as a light meal.

## STUFFED PYZY

Pyzy are made from raw potato, bound with cooked potato. I have used half and half to achieve a fairly light, well bound result; but more raw potato ought to be used, necessitating longer cooking. They take slightly longer to cook than the other dumplings but have a different flavour and texture that warrants the method; I find them slightly more filling to eat.
I have used a cooked meat filling – a raw meat filling may be used but the dumplings would take even longer to cook and there is a danger of the potato mixture disintegrating. You may use other fillings equally successfully. Try any of the others used in this chapter. Serves 4 (8 dumplings).

*2 potatoes, total weight 1 lb / 500 g / 1 lb*

*¼ cup / 25 g / 1 oz plain flour (all purpose flour)*

*salt and freshly ground black pepper*

**FILLING**

*½ cup / 100 g / 4 oz cooked meat, minced (ground)*

*½ small onion, grated*

*2–3 tbsp good stock or gravy*

**TO SERVE**

*½ cup / 100 g / 4 oz bacon fat or rindless streaky bacon (slices), diced*

*a little fat or butter*

Boil one potato in its skin until tender – about 20 minutes. Drain, cool, then peel. Rub the potato through a sieve. Peel and grate the second potato. Rinse it and squeeze all the water from the shreds. Mix the cooked and uncooked potato with the flour, ½ tsp salt and some pepper. Beat the mixture well so that it combines to a soft dough.

Mix the ingredients for the filling. Divide the potato mixture into eight. Flour your hands, take a portion of potato and flatten it on the palm of your hand into a patty. Place an eighth of the filling on the patty, then mould the potato around it to enclose it completely. The outside of the dumpling should be smooth and the mixture should feel firmly bound together. This can be achieved by gently moulding. Shape the other dumplings in the same way.

Bring a saucepan of water to simmering point. Cook the dumplings at a steady simmer for 5–7 minutes. The pyzy will rise to the surface when cooked. They should look slightly glossy and feel firm. If any of the shreds of potato begin to separate from the dumplings, they are overcooking and will disintegrate soon, so lift them out of the water immediately.

While the dumplings are cooking, brown the bacon in the fat. Transfer the dumplings to a warmed serving dish and top with the bacon and fat. Serve at once.

## PIEROGI

Similar to Italian ravioli, pierogi are delicious. I also found that they reminded me of some of the Chinese dumplings served as dim sum. However, they do have a character and flavour of their own. I include two fillings – make only one as the quantities will fill the whole batch of dough. Both may be served as a main course. Serves 4–6 (about 65 pierogi).

*2 cups / 225 g / 8 oz plain flour (all purpose flour)*

*salt and freshly ground black pepper*

*1 egg*

*⅜ cup / 75 ml / 3 fl oz water*

*beaten egg to seal*

**MEAT FILLING**

*1 small onion, very finely chopped*

*2 tbsp / 25 g / 1 oz fat or butter*

*1¼ cups / 275 g / 10 oz cooked pork, minced (ground)*

*2 tbsp stock*

**CHEESE FILLING**

*1½ cups / 350 g / 12 oz cottage cheese*

*2 cups / 75 g / 3 oz fresh breadcrumbs*

*2 egg yolks*

**TOPPING**

*½ lb / 225 g / 8 oz bacon fat or rindless streaky bacon (slices), diced*

*a little fat or butter*

Sift the flour into a bowl with ½ tsp salt. Make a well in the middle, then add the egg and water. Mix the flour in to make a firm dough. Use your hands to knead the dough together in the bowl. Turn out the dough on to a surface and knead well until smooth. Divide the dough into quarters and wrap in cling film (plastic wrap) while you prepare the chosen filling.

For the meat filling, cook the onion in the fat or butter until soft – about 10 minutes. Add the remaining ingredients and season to taste.

For the cheese filling, strain the cottage cheese to remove as much liquid as possible. Mix with the remaining ingredients and season to taste.

On a lightly floured surface, roll out a quarter of the dough into a round measuring about 28–30 cm / 11–12 in across. The dough should be quite thin. Using a biscuit (cookie) cutter, cut out 6 cm / 2½ in rounds. Use a teaspoon to place a little of the chosen filling on each round. Brush the edges of the dough with beaten egg, then fold the dough over to enclose the filling into semi-circular dumplings. Pinch the edges of the dough together firmly to seal in the filling. Re-roll all the dough trimmings. Roll, cut and fill the remaining dough.

Cook the pierogi in a large saucepan of steadily boiling salted water or stock for about 4 minutes. While the pierogi are cooking, brown the bacon in the fat. Drain the pierogi, transfer them to a warmed serving dish and top with the bacon and fat. If the pierogi are cooked in stock, then ladle just a little stock over them.

## PIEROGI RUSKA

These are inexpensive and delicious – two good reasons for being particularly popular. Serves 4–6 (about 65 pierogi).

| |
|---|
| *Pierogi dough (see previous recipe)* |
| ***FILLING*** |
| *¾ lb / 350 g / 12 oz potato* |
| *1 small onion, grated* |
| *2 tbsp / 25 g / 1 oz butter* |
| *1 cup / 175 g / 6 oz cottage cheese* |
| *salt and freshly ground black pepper* |
| *bacon fat or bacon to serve (see previous recipe)* |

Prepare the dough following the recipe instructions. For the filling, boil the potato in its skin until tender – about 20 minutes. Drain, cool, then peel. Rub the potato through a sieve.

Cook the grated onion in the butter for 5 minutes, stirring all the time, then add it to the potato. Strain as much liquid as possible from the cottage cheese. Rub it through a sieve and add to the potato. Mix well with seasoning to taste.

Roll out the dough as in the previous recipe, cutting and filling the pierogi in the same way. Follow the cooking and serving instructions using water instead of stock for cooking. Make sure that the pierogi are piping hot when served.

## PRAZUCHA

I have added some soured cream to enrich this gruel. It makes an easy, fairly stodgy supper dish which is filling but boring. Serves 4.

| |
|---|
| *1 cup / 225 g / 8 oz cottage cheese* |
| *2 cups / 225 g / 8 oz buckwheat flour* |
| *2½ cups / 600 ml / 1 pt water* |
| *salt and freshly ground black pepper* |
| *⅔ cup / 150 ml / ¼ pt soured cream* |
| *¼ cup / 50 g / 2 oz butter* |
| *4 tbsp snipped chives* |

Place the cottage cheese in scalded muslin (cheesecloth) and squeeze as much liquid as possible out of it. When squeezed, the cheese should be far drier and crumbly. Set aside.

Place the flour in a non-stick or heavy-based saucepan and gradually stir in the water. Add a little seasoning. Bring to the boil, stirring all the time, until very thick. Cook gently for about 3 minutes. Stir in the soured cream and continue to cook, stirring, until the mixture forms a thick porridge that holds its shape. Taste and adjust the seasoning.

Melt the butter and dip a metal spoon into it. Use to scoop the prazucha in neat portions on to warmed plates. Top with the crumbled cottage cheese and chives. Serve at once.

PRAZUCHA

## KASHA WITH APPLE

Plain cooked buckwheat, perhaps with a little melted butter or fat poured over, is a popular accompaniment on the Polish menu. Follow the instructions in this recipe for cooking buckwheat to serve as a plain vegetable, the addition of apple and onion complements its deliciously nutty flavour. Serves 4.

*1 cup/175 g/6 oz roasted buckwheat*

*2 cups/475 ml/16 fl oz water*

*salt and freshly ground black pepper*

*1 large onion*

*¼ cup/50 g/2 oz butter or fat*

*½ lb/225 g/8 oz cooking apple, peeled, cored and diced*

*4 tbsp snipped chives or chopped fresh parsley*

Place the buckwheat in a sieve and rinse under cold running water. Place in a saucepan with the water and a little salt. Heat gently until just boiling, then remove the pan from the heat. Cover tightly and leave for 30 minutes by which time the buckwheat should have absorbed all the water.

Cook the onion in the butter for about 15 minutes, until thoroughly softened. Stir in the apple and continue to cook for 5 minutes. Turn this mixture on to the cooked buckwheat and gently fork it into the grains with the chives. Serve at once.

KASHA WITH APPLE

LASANKI WITH CABBAGE

## LASANKI WITH CABBAGE

Małgosia explained that when she was a child, łasanki was very much a storecupboard dish, made when there was nothing else for supper. They are tiny squares of pasta, boiled and served as an accompaniment to a main dish, tossed with some soured cream or mixed with vegetables as here. Serves 4.

*3 cups/350 g/12 oz plain flour (all purpose flour)*

*salt and freshly ground black pepper*

*2 eggs*

*⅔ cup/150 ml/¼ pt water*

*1½ lb/675 g/1½ lb green cabbage, trimmed of tough stalk and shredded*

*1 large onion, thinly sliced*

*¼ cup/50 g/2 oz butter or fat*

*1 tsp caraway seeds*

*1 clove garlic, crushed (optional)*

Sift the flour into a bowl with ½ tsp salt. Make a well in the middle, then add the eggs and water. Gradually stir the flour into the liquid. Use your hand to gather the dough together, then knead until it is smooth. Cut the dough in half and wrap one piece in cling film (plastic wrap).

Roll out the remaining dough on a lightly floured surface into a 35.5 cm/14 in square. Dust with a little flour, fold in half and cut into thin strips. These should be 0.5–1 cm/¼–½ in wide. Cut across them to make tiny squares. Dust these łazanki with a little flour and sprinkle on a large plate. Repeat with the remaining dough.

Cook the cabbage in boiling salted water for 3–4 minutes, then drain. Cook the onion in the butter with the caraway and garlic, if used, until soft – about 15 minutes.

Cook the łazanki in a saucepan of boiling salted water for 4 minutes, then drain. Stir the cabbage into the onion and heat for 1 minute. Mix in the łazanki and transfer the mixture to a warmed serving dish. Serve at once.

## CHERRY PIEROZKI

Other small fruits may be used instead of cherries. For example, try raspberries, blackberries, small or halved strawberries, or blueberries. Serves 6 (about 32 pierozki).

*1½ cups/175 g/6 oz plain flour (all purpose flour)*

*1 egg*

*¼–⅜ cup/50–75 ml/2–3 fl oz water*

*½ lb/225 g/8 oz cherries, stoned (pitted)*

*icing sugar (confectioners' sugar) to dredge*

*soured cream to serve (optional)*

Sift the flour into a bowl. Make a well in the middle, then add the egg and water. Mix the ingredients into a firm dough. Knead well until smooth. Roll out the dough into a round measuring about 40 cm/16 in across. Cut rounds of dough, using a 6 cm/2½ in round biscuit (cookie) cutter. Place a cherry on a round of dough, then fold the dough in half to enclose the cherry completely. Pinch the edges together firmly to seal in the fruit. Fill and seal all the dumplings, re-rolling all the dough trimmings.

Cook the pierozki in a saucepan of boiling water for about 3 minutes. Drain well and serve dredged with icing sugar (confectioners' sugar). Soured cream may be served with the pierozki.

## PLUM KNEDLE

A family meal in Poland does not necessarily consist of a main course followed by pudding; sweet dishes, such as this one, may be served as a light meal on their own. Other fruit may be used instead of the plums: try lightly poached chunks of cooking apple, hulled strawberries or stoned (pitted) cherries. The knedle may also be filled with jam or marmalade. Serves 4 (12 knedle).

*knedle dough (page 61)*

*12 ripe plums*

*¼ cup/50 g/2 oz unsalted butter, melted*

*icing sugar (confectioners' sugar) to dust*

Prepare the knedle dough as described in the recipe. Divide it into 12 pieces. Remove the stalks from the plums but leave the fruit whole.

Lightly flour your hands and flatten a portion of dough into a neat patty on your palm. Place a plum in the middle, then ease the dough around it to enclose completely.

Cook the plum knedle in a saucepan of steadily boiling water for about 3 minutes, until the dumplings are cooked. Drain and serve at once, with the butter poured over and dusted with icing sugar (confectioners' sugar).

**NOTE:** Warmed honey is also good with the plums instead of icing sugar.

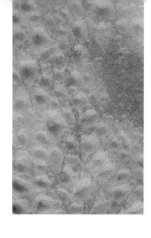

# 7

# PANCAKES AND BREADS

Polish rye bread, flavoured with caraway seeds, is readily available but I include a recipe because the homemade version tastes so good. As well as rye bread, a flat wholewheat bread is baked and white bread is also prepared. A rich plait of white bread, probably served for breakfast, is included in this chapter.

Filled and coated Polish pancakes are particularly good, with a crisp outer coating to provide an excellent contrast in texture compared with the softer stuffing. The basic pancakes are not unusual but the ways in which they are served are a little different. Apart from the savoury fillings, soft cheese, poached fruit, fruit syrups or preserved fruits complement the pancakes. Look out for Eva's recipe for apple pancakes – they are irresistible.

However, the real diet-killer in this chapter must be the mouthwatering doughnuts. Polish doughnuts are particularly light and they are glazed with icing. The traditional filling is rose preserve made from the petals of a particular type of scented climbing rose. Unfortunately I could not purchase any and was advised by the lady in the delicatessen that this preserve has been too expensive to purchase for a good many years. So, next summer, with Eva's advice on selecting the roses, I shall make some at home, which is apparently the more common means of obtaining the preserve in Poland than by buying it. I am told that the roses are cooked with sugar, in very much the same way as for jam-making, and that the product is a thick conserve which does not set in the same way as fruit jams.

## PLAITED BREAD

A rich bread that is popular for breakfast. Makes 1 loaf.

*2 tsp (active) dried yeast or 20 g/¾ oz fresh yeast (¾ cake compressed yeast)*

*½ cup/100 ml/4 fl oz warm milk*

*1 tsp sugar*

*3 cups/350 g/12 oz strong plain flour (hard wheat flour)*

*1 tsp salt*

*¼ cup/50 g/2 oz butter*

*1 egg*

*beaten egg to glaze*

Sprinkle the dried yeast over the milk and sugar. Cream the fresh yeast with the milk and sugar. Leave in a warm place until frothy. Place the flour and salt in a bowl. Rub in the butter and make a well in the middle. Add the egg and yeast liquid and beat together. Mix in the flour to make a firm dough.

Knead the dough into a ball, then turn out on to a surface. Knead well for about 10 minutes, until smooth and elastic. Put the dough back into the bowl and cover with cling film (plastic wrap). Leave to rise in a warm place until doubled in size – about 1½–2 hours.

Turn out the dough and knead it lightly. Divide into three equal portions. Roll each portion into a long sausage measuring about 40 cm/6 in. Grease a large baking sheet and lift the strips on to it, pinching their ends together. Plait the strips into a neat loaf. The plait must not be too tight nor too loose. Cover loosely with cling film and leave to rise in a warm place until doubled in size. Meanwhile, set the oven at 220°C/425°F/gas 7.

Brush the loaf with beaten egg. Bake for about 30 minutes, until glossy, brown and cooked through. Check that the loaf is browned underneath and that it sounds hollow when tapped on the base. Cool on a wire rack and store in an airtight container.

## BUCHTY

These versatile rolls are of German origin but they are a popular Polish bread. They may be served in a number of ways: as a rich bread for breakfast, hot with fruit syrup or bottled fruit as a sweet dish, or the rolls may be filled with some fruit conserve or marmalade as they are shaped. When Małgosia tasted my efforts, she also mentioned that the cooled rolls may be sliced and toasted or baked until golden to make crisp rusks for serving with smoked meats. I thought they made a delicious dessert with fruit syrup. They were certainly worth the hard work involved in the hand-beating of the dough. You will need a strong arm for this recipe! Makes 16.

PLAITED BREAD

BUCHTY

3 tsp (active) dried yeast or 25 g/1 oz fresh yeast (1 cake compressed yeast)

½ cup/100 ml/4 fl oz warm milk

6 tbsp/75 g/3 oz sugar

4 cups/500 g/1 lb strong plain flour (hard wheat flour)

1 tsp salt

10 tbsp/150 g/5 oz butter

3 eggs

icing sugar (confectioners' sugar) to dredge

preserved fruit or fruit syrup to serve

Sprinkle the dried yeast over the milk and 1 tsp of the sugar. Cream the fresh yeast with the milk and 1 tsp of the sugar. Leave in a warm place until frothy. Place the flour and salt in a bowl and make a well in the middle. Melt 6 tbsp/75 g/3 oz of the butter and pour it into the flour with the eggs. Add the yeast liquid and beat the liquids together. Gradually work in the flour to form a very soft dough. The mixture is a cross between a batter and a dough: too stiff to beat with a spoon, too wet to knead.

Wash and dry your hands in hot water and beat the mixture with the palm of one hand. Once you get the hang of it the process is not too bad. As the mixture develops it becomes elastic and tends not to stick to your hand. Carry on beating the mixture for about 15 minutes, by which time it should be coming cleanly away from the bowl as you work it. It should not be too sticky. Cover with cling film (plastic wrap) and leave to rise in a warm place until doubled in size – about 2 hours.

Thoroughly grease and base line an 18 cm/7 in square deep cake tin. Melt the remaining butter. When the mixture has risen, beat it back slightly with a spoon. Moisten your hand with butter and take a portion of the dough about the size of a small tomato. (The dough should be divided into 16 portions but this is too difficult so you have to use a certain amount of judgement.) Gently mould the dough into a small, round roll, then place it in the prepared tin. Keep your hand buttered while shaping the remaining dough into 15 more small rolls. Place them in the tin, slightly apart, in neat rows. Cover with cling film and leave to rise in a warm place until they just cover the base of the tin. Meanwhile, set the oven at 180°C/350°F/gas 4.

Pour the remaining melted butter all over the rolls, Bake for 30–35 minutes, until risen and browned. Turn out and break off rolls to serve hot with fruit syrup or bottled fruit. Leave any leftover rolls to cool on a wire rack.

## RYE BREAD

Use this as a base for canapés, or serve it very thinly sliced and buttered with herring spread (page 14) to go with well-chilled Polish vodka. Makes 1 loaf.

*2 tsp (active) dried yeast or 20 g/¾ oz fresh yeast (¾ cake compressed yeast)*

*½ cup/100 ml/4 fl oz warm milk*

*1 tsp sugar*

*2 cups/225 g/8 oz strong white flour (hard wheat flour)*

*2 cups/225 g/8 oz rye flour*

*1 tbsp caraway seeds*

*½ tsp salt*

*½ cup/100 ml/4 fl oz warm water*

Sprinkle the dried yeast over the milk and sugar. Cream the fresh yeast with the milk and sugar. Leave in a warm place until frothy. Mix both types of flour in a large bowl. Stir in the caraway seeds and salt, then make a well in the middle. Pour the yeast liquid into the flour. Add the water and mix to form a firm dough.

Knead in the bowl, then turn the dough out on to a surface. Knead thoroughly for about 10 minutes, until smooth and elastic. Put the dough back in the bowl and cover with cling film (plastic wrap). Leave to rise in a warm place until doubled in size. This will take about 2 hours.

Turn out the dough and knead it lightly. Shape into an oval loaf and place it on a greased baking sheet. Cover loosely with cling film and leave to rise in a warm place, again until doubled in size. This second proving will take about 1 hour. Meanwhile, set the oven at 220°C/425°F/gas 7.

Brush the bread with a little water. Bake for 30–35 minutes, until lightly browned and cooked through. To test if the loaf is cooked, it will sound hollow when tapped on the base. Cool on a wire rack and store in an airtight container.

## DOUGHNUTS

Paczki in Polish, these are simply wonderful! Małgosia told me of a Warsaw pâtisserie by the name of Blikle, that is renowned for its doughnuts and other specialities. Apparently, they actually export their doughnuts to those customers who can afford to pay for this service. Polish doughnuts should be very light with a little preserve made of rose petals in the centre; however plum spread made with the minimum of sugar (available from Polish delicatessens or good continental shops) may be used instead. I used tangy homemade plum jam and the results were excellent. The dough is not an easy one to work as it is quite soft but the results are particularly light. Makes 25 small doughnuts.

*3 tsp (active) dried yeast or 25 g/1 oz fresh yeast (1 cake compressed yeast)*

*4 tbsp warm water*

*1 tsp sugar*

*3 cups/350 g/12 oz strong white flour (hard wheat flour)*

*¼ cup/50 g/2 oz butter, melted*

*1 egg*

*grated rind of ½ lemon (optional)*

*2 tbsp/25 g/1 oz caster (superfine) sugar*

*⅜ cup/75 ml/3 fl oz warm milk*

*about 5 tbsp plum jam or spread*

*sunflower oil to deep fry*

*boiled icing (boiled frosting) (page 85) or icing sugar (confectioners' sugar) to coat*

Sprinkle the dried yeast over the water and the 1 tsp of sugar. Cream the fresh yeast with the water and the 1 tsp sugar. Leave in a warm place until frothy. Place the flour in a bowl and make a well in the middle. Add the butter, egg, lemon rind, caster (superfine) sugar and milk, then stir in the yeast liquid. Gradually work in the flour to make a soft dough. Knead the dough together in the bowl.

The dough is very soft and it should be worked quickly and constantly to prevent it sticking to the work surface, so only turn it out of the bowl when you are ready to knead it vigorously. Lightly flour the surface and knead the dough, keeping it moving and adding as little extra flour as possible. After a few minutes, the dough becomes elastic and the kneading is easier. Continue for about 15 minutes, until the dough is very smooth, light and elastic. Replace it in the bowl and cover with cling film (plastic wrap). Leave to rise in a warm place until doubled in size – about 2 hours.

Dredge a number of baking sheets with flour. Turn out the dough and knead it lightly. Sprinkle a little flour on the surface and roll out the dough fairly thinly. Use a 5 cm/2 in round cutter to cut rounds of dough, re-rolling all the trimmings. You should have about 50 rounds. Place a little preserve on a round of dough and press a second round on top, stretching the edges together and pinching them firmly to seal in the filling. Place on the floured baking sheets. When all the doughnuts are cut and filled, cover them loosely with cling film or plastic. Leave them in a warm place to rise – this should take up to 30 minutes.

Heat the oil for deep frying to 160°C/325°F. It is important that the oil does not rise above 180°C/350°F during cooking or the doughnuts will brown and crisp before they are cooked through. The lower cooking temperature allows the doughnuts to puff up before they set firm. Cook a few at a time, turning each one once to brown both sides. When puffed and golden, drain on absorbent kitchen paper.

The doughnuts may be coated with icing (frosting) or dredged with icing sugar (confectioners' sugar). They are delicious while warm.

## NALESNIKI

Here is the basic recipe for pancakes. They may be served with fruit syrups, fruit bottled in syrup or liqueur, with marmalade or with plum spread. Makes 8.

| |
|---|
| *1 cup/100 g/4 oz plain flour (all purpose flour)* |
| *1 egg* |
| *½ cup/100 ml/4 fl oz water* |
| *½ cup/100 ml/4 fl oz milk* |
| *oil or butter to cook* |

Sift the flour into a bowl and make a well in the middle. Add the egg and about a third of the water. Beat the egg and water, gradually working in the flour and adding more water with the milk to make a smooth batter. Leave to stand for 30 minutes. You may have to thin the batter with a little extra water if it thickens a great deal on standing.

Heat a large frying pan (skillet) and grease it lightly. Ladle some of the batter on to it, rolling the pan to ensure the base is evenly coated. Cook the pancake over a medium heat until golden underneath and fairly dry. Use a spatula or large palette knife

DOUGHNUTS

NALEŚNIKI

(metal spatula) to loosen the edges, then turn the pancake over and cook the second side. Repeat with the remaining batter. Place absorbent kitchen paper between the pancakes as you stack them to prevent them sticking together.

Spread the pancakes with the chosen filling and fold into quarters. Top with fruit syrup or preserved fruit and serve with soured cream.

**NOTE:** The pancakes freeze well when cool. Pack them interleaved with freezer film so that a few may be lifted off without having to thaw the whole batch. Heat them individually in a greased pan or use for stuffed pancakes.

## SAVOURY FILLED PANCAKES

Select either of these fillings to stuff eight pancakes. Serves 4.

8 pancakes (see Naleśniki, previous recipe)

oil or butter to cook

**CABBAGE FILLING**

¾ lb/350 g/12 oz green cabbage, trimmed of tough stalk

salt and freshly ground black pepper

6 slices/100 g/4 oz rindless smoked streaky bacon, diced

½ tsp caraway seeds

4 tbsp drained sauerkraut

2 tbsp soured cream

**MEAT FILLING**

1 onion, finely chopped

2 tbsp/25 g/1 oz butter

½ tsp dried marjoram

2 tbsp chopped fresh parsley

1½ cups/350 g/12 oz cooked meat, minced (ground)

4 tbsp soured cream

**COATING**

1 egg, beaten

1 cup/75 g/3 oz dry white breadcrumbs

Prepare the pancakes before making the chosen filling. For the cabbage filling, cook the cabbage in lightly salted boiling water for 5–7 minutes, until soft. Drain well, then cool and squeeze all the water from the cabbage. Chop the cabbage finely.

Cook the bacon in a heavy-based pan until the fat runs, then continue to cook, stirring, until browned. Mix the cabbage, bacon, caraway, sauerkraut and soured cream with seasoning to taste.

For the meat filling, cook the onion in the butter for 10 minutes. Add the marjoram, parsley and meat. Stir in the soured cream to moisten the mixture and add seasoning to taste.

Divide the chosen filling into eight portions. Lay a pancake on a board and place a portion of filling in the middle. Fold one end of the pancake over the filling, then brush the pancake with beaten egg. Fold the sides over and lastly fold the end over to enclose the filling in a neat parcel. Brush all over with egg and coat with breadcrumbs. Repeat with the remaining pancakes and filling.

Heat a little oil or butter in a large frying pan (skillet) and cook the pancakes, turning once until the coating is golden. Serve at once.

## GRIDDLE PANCAKES

These are made of an unusual dough containing cottage cheese. Serve them hot, as they are hard and chewy when cold. Makes about 20.

½ cup / 100 g / 4 oz cottage cheese

2 eggs

2 tbsp / 25 g / 1 oz sugar

½ tsp natural vanilla essence (flavoring)

grated rind of ½ lemon (optional)

2 cups / 225 g / 8 oz plain flour (all purpose flour)

2 tsp baking powder

butter to grease

icing sugar (confectioners' sugar) to dredge

soured cream to serve

Sieve the cottage cheese into a bowl, then beat in the eggs, sugar, vanilla and lemon rind. Sift the flour and baking powder into the mixture and stir to make a soft dough.

Turn out the dough on to a lightly floured surface and knead lightly. Roll out to 1 cm / ½ in thick and cut out 6 cm / 2½ in rounds. Re-roll the trimmings.

Heat a griddle and grease it with a little butter. Place the pancakes on the griddle, slightly apart to allow for spreading. Cook over a medium heat until the pancakes are golden underneath. Turn and cook the second sides until golden. Serve at once, dredged with icing sugar (confectioners' sugar) and topped with soured cream.

## APPLE PANCAKES

These are Eva's speciality and they are so more-ish that once tried they are not easily forgotten! The great surprise is that they are really quick and easy to make too. Makes 10.

½ cup / 50 g / 2 oz plain flour (all purpose flour)

2 tbsp caster sugar (superfine sugar)

1 egg, separated

4 tbsp soured cream

½ lb / 225 g / 8 oz cooking apples, peeled, cored and finely sliced

butter to cook

icing sugar (confectioners' sugar) to dredge

soured cream to serve (optional)

Sift the flour into a bowl. Stir in the sugar, egg yolk and soured cream to make a thick batter. Add the apples, stirring for a while without breaking the slices. Whisk the egg white until standing in stiff peaks. Fold it into the apple mixture, making sure it is well combined with the ingredients.

Heat a little butter in a large frying pan (skillet) or griddle. Drop spoonfuls of the apple mixture on to the hot surface. Use the spoon to arrange the mixture in fairly thin, neat rounds measuring about 6–7.5 cm / 2½–3 in across. Cook fairly slowly until golden underneath and almost set on top. Turn the pancakes over and cook the second side until golden. Serve at once, dredged with sugar, with some soured cream, if liked.

# 8

# DESSERTS

This is not an extensive chapter because desserts do not feature at the end of ordinary meals. Sweet foods, like fruit dumplings or pancakes, are just as likely to form the main part of a family meal as a savoury dish.

In some of these recipes, and many more of those in the following chapter, you will find significant quantities of poppy seeds used in a ground form. It is important to buy poppy seeds from a good continental shop (or a Polish delicatessen if possible) where they will be fresh and sweet. I spent time preparing desserts and cakes that were ruined by the bitter flavour of poppy seeds purchased in jars from two separate supermarkets. The glossary includes advice on grinding the seeds.

Pancakes, fruit dumplings, doughnuts and buchty are other recipes to serve for the sweet course, all to be found in the relevant chapters.

## POPPY SEED PUDDING

You will definitely have to find a good source of poppy seeds to achieve success with this pudding. It is deliciously nutty. Serves 6.

*¼ lb/100 g/4 oz poppy seeds, ground (page 11)*

*4 eggs, separated*

*½ cup/100 g/4 oz caster sugar (superfine sugar)*

*½ cup/100 g/4 oz ground almonds*

*½ cup/100 ml/4 fl oz milk*

*1⅓ cups/50 g/2 oz fresh breadcrumbs*

*⅔ cup/100 g/4 oz good quality candied orange peel, chopped*

*icing sugar (confectioners' sugar) to dredge*

*candied orange slices to decorate (optional)*

*soured cream to serve*

Prepare a large saucepan of boiling water and a steamer. Base-line and grease an 18–20 cm/7–8 in soufflé dish. Ensure that the poppy seeds are thoroughly ground.

Cream the egg yolks with the sugar in a bowl until pale and thick. Stir in the poppy seeds, almonds and milk. Add the breadcrumbs and candied orange peel, mixing well. Whisk the egg whites until stiff and fold them into the mixture. Turn the mixture into the prepared dish. Cover with greased greaseproof (waxed) paper and double-thick foil. Crimp the edges of the foil firmly around the edge of the dish or tie it down with string to exclude all steam.

Steam the pudding over boiling water for 1¼ hours, until risen and firm. Turn the pudding out on to a double thick clean tea towel and remove the lining paper from the base. Invert the pudding on to a warmed serving platter and dredge the top with icing sugar (confectioners' sugar). Arrange a few candied orange slices on or around the pudding if you like, then serve at once. Soured cream goes well with the pudding or a vanilla custard may be served (see note).

**NOTE:** This is an easy vanilla custard to make: blend 3 tbsp cornflour (cornstarch) and 3–4 tbsp sugar with a little cold milk from 2½ cups/600 ml/1 pt. Heat the remaining milk, then stir it into the paste. Return to the pan and bring to the boil. Simmer for 3–4 minutes. Stir in 1 tsp natural vanilla essence (flavoring). Remove the pan from the heat and beat in 6 egg yolks. Heat again until thickened, without boiling, then serve.

## BAKED BUCKWHEAT PUDDING

The addition of dried fruits and lemon rind lifts an old-fashioned and inexpensive pudding. Serve vanilla custard (see note below) with the pudding or offer a warmed fruit syrup or honey instead. Serves 6.

*4 eggs, separated*

*½ cup/100 g/4 oz caster sugar (superfine sugar)*

*1 tsp natural vanilla essence (flavoring)*

*scant 1 cup/200 ml/7 fl oz soured cream*

*grated rind of 1 lemon*

*½ cup/75 g/3 oz raisins*

*⅔ cup/100 g/4 oz candied peel*

*1¾ cups/225 g/8 oz buckwheat flour*

*icing sugar (confectioners' sugar) to dredge*

Set the oven at 180°C/350°F/gas 4. Base-line and grease an 18–20 cm/7–8 in charlotte mould or deep round tin.

Cream the egg yolks, sugar and vanilla in a bowl until pale and thick. Beat in the soured cream, lemon rind and fruit, then stir in the buckwheat flour. Whisk the egg whites until stiff and fold them into the mixture using a metal spoon. Take care to keep the mixture light. Turn the pudding into the prepared mould or tin.

Bake for 1¼ hours, until risen and browned. Check the pudding about 8 minutes before the end of cooking and cover loosely with a piece of foil if it is likely to become too dark. Turn out the pudding on to a clean tea towel, remove the lining paper, and invert the pudding on to a warmed serving dish. Dredge with icing sugar (confectioners' sugar) and serve.

KRAKÓW: FLOWER SELLERS IN FRONT OF THE OLD CLOTH HALL.

NOODLES WITH POPPY SEEDS

## NOODLES WITH POPPY SEEDS

This was part of the traditional Polish Christmas eve meal, although other desserts have replaced it in some households. Serves 6.

*2 cups/225 g/8 oz plain flour (all purpose flour)*

*½ tsp salt*

*1 egg*

*3 tbsp water*

*2 tbsp/25 g/1 oz butter, melted*

*3 tbsp clear honey*

*⅓ cup/50 g/2 oz poppy seeds, ground (page 11)*

Sift the flour and salt into a bowl and make a well in the middle. Add the egg and water, beating the two together. Mix in the flour to make a very stiff dough. Gradually knead the dough into a ball. Turn out on to a surface and knead until smooth. Cut the dough in half and wrap one piece in cling film (plastic wrap).

Roll out the second piece into an oblong measuring 30 × 18 cm/12 × 7 in, dust with flour and fold in half. Cut across the fold into thin noodles, measuring 0.5–1 cm/¼–½ in wide. Dust the noodles with a little flour and shake them on to a plate. Repeat with the remaining dough.

Cook the noodles in plenty of boiling water for about 4 minutes, until tender but not soft. Drain and toss with the melted butter, honey and poppy seeds. Serve hot.

## LAMAŃCE

This is another traditional sweet dish for serving at the Christmas eve feast. Lamańce means broken, reflecting the fact that some of the biscuits (cookies) are broken in the dip or that they should not be quite so perfect in shape. Makes 64.

| |
|---|
| 1½ cups/175 g/6 oz plain flour (all purpose flour) |
| 2 tbsp/25 g/1 oz butter |
| scant ½ cup/50 g/2 oz icing sugar (confectioners' sugar) |
| 1 egg yolk |
| 3 tbsp soured cream |
| **DIP** |
| ⅔ cup/100 g/4 oz poppy seeds, ground (page 11) |
| ¼ cup/50 g/2 oz ground almonds |
| 2 tbsp honey |
| 1¼ cups/300 ml/½ pt soured cream |

Grease several baking sheets. Sift the flour into a bowl and rub in the butter. Stir in the sugar, egg yolk and soured cream to make a soft dough. Cut the dough in half and wrap in cling film (plastic wrap). Chill for about 15 minutes, or until firm enough to roll out.

Set the oven at 180°C/350°F/gas 4. Roll out half the dough to an oblong measuring 20 × 40 cm/8 × 16 in, then cut this into four 10 cm/4 in squares. Cut the squares in half diagonally to make triangles. Repeat with the second piece of dough. Place the biscuits (cookies) on the baking sheets. Bake for about 8–12 minutes, until golden. Cool on wire racks.

For the dip, mix the ingredients together, then lightly crush about four of the biscuits into it. Mix well, then offer the biscuits to dip into the creamy mixture.

## KUTIA

This wheat 'porridge' is apparently of Russian origin but in Poland it is one of the 12 traditional dishes for Christmas eve. The kutia is flavoured with poppy seeds and enriched with thick cream. Serves 6.

| |
|---|
| ¾ cup/175 g/6 oz wheat grain (not cracked) |
| 3¾ cups/900 ml/1½ pt water |
| pinch of salt |
| ⅔ cup/100 g/4 oz poppy seeds, ground (page 11) |
| 4–6 tbsp clear honey |
| 1¼ cups/300 ml/½ pt double cream (heavy cream) |
| about ½ cup/50 g/2 oz blanched almonds, cut into slivers and toasted |

Place the wheat in a sieve and rinse under cold running water. Bring a large saucepan of water to the boil, add the wheat and bring the water back to the boil. Cook for 1 minute, then drain the wheat. Put the blanched wheat and measured water in the top of a double boiler or in a bowl over a saucepan of just boiling water. Cover the wheat mixture closely and cook for about 7 hours, until it has absorbed all the water. Stir the mixture frequently to soften the grain and remember to top up the boiling water in the saucepan. Pound the cooked wheat with the back of a wooden spoon to break down the soft grain. Set aside to cool.

Stir the poppy seeds and honey into the wheat (add the smaller amount of honey at this stage). Whip the cream lightly until thick and standing in peaks. Lightly fold the cream into the kutia. Taste and add more honey, if required. Chill briefly before serving topped with the almonds.

LAMAŃCE

remaining filo. Sprinkle the breadcrumbs over the pastry, leaving a 2.5–3.5 cm/1–1½ in border. Spread the apple mixture all over the breadcrumbs. Fold the border of pastry over the edge of the apples, then roll up the pastry and its filling from the long side. Use the cloth to help roll the strudel. Lift the strudel in the cloth (this is its real purpose in this recipe) and roll it on to the tin, so that the pastry join is underneath. Gently pat the strudel into shape and brush it all over with the remaining butter.

Bake for 30–40 minutes, taking care that it does not become too brown. Serve the strudel hot, dredged with icing sugar (confectioners' sugar). You will need two large fish slices and a serving platter or board if you intend to serve the strudel whole.

**NOTE:** Always keep filo pastry covered with cling film (plastic wrap) while you work, as it dries rapidly and crumbles into bits if allowed to lay uncovered in the air. Also, make sure the surface is absolutely dry as spots of water will cause the pastry to become sticky and break. If you do not have a large tin, then curve the strudel on a baking sheet.

## APPLE STRUDEL

Strudel is popular all over Eastern Europe, and in Poland it may well be served as one of the sweet dishes for the Christmas eve meal. I'm afraid I have opted out of making strudel pastry and used bought filo. Serves 8.

*2 lb/1 kg/2 lb cooking apples, peeled, cored and roughly chopped*

*½ cup/100 g/4 oz caster sugar (superfine sugar)*

*1 tsp ground cinnamon*

*pinch of ground allspice*

*½ cup/75 g/3 oz raisins*

*6 sheets filo pastry*

*¼ cup/50 g/2 oz butter, melted*

*1⅓ cups/50 g/2 oz fresh breadcrumbs*

*icing sugar (confectioners' sugar) to dust*

Set the oven at 190°C/375°F/gas 5. Grease a large roasting tin. Lay a clean cloth on a work surface. Mix the apples, sugar, spices and raisins.

Lay two sheets of filo pastry on the cloth, overlapping them by about 5 cm/2 in along the long side. Brush very lightly with a little butter, then top with two more sheets, butter and top with the

## DRIED FRUIT COMPÔTE

Another sweet recipe for serving as part of the Christmas eve menu. The compôte may include any dried fruits that are available. The fruits are steeped in a thick, sweet syrup. Serves 8.

*1½ lb/675 g/1½ lb dried fruit, such as prunes, apricots, pears, peaches, apples, raisins*

*¾ cup/175 g/6 oz sugar*

*pared rind and juice of 2 lemons*

*pared rind and juice of 1 orange*

*about ½ cup/50 g/2 oz blanched almonds, cut into slivers and toasted*

Place the fruit in a bowl and pour in enough water to cover the fruit well. Cover and leave to soak overnight.

Next day, drain the liquid from the fruit into a saucepan and add the sugar, fruit rind and juices. Bring to the boil, then add the soaked fruit and simmer for 3–5 minutes, until the fruit is tender. Drain, reserving the liquid, and place the fruit in a bowl. Return the fruit rind and liquid to the pan and bring to the boil. Boil the syrup until reduced and thickened slightly. Strain the syrup over the fruit. Leave until cold before serving topped with the almonds.

FRUIT SALAD

## FRUIT SALAD

A family sweet to make the most of seasonal fruit.
The ingredients may be varied to include whatever is
available. Serves 6.

pared rind and juice of 1 lemon

2 oranges

2 eating apples, peeled, cored and thickly sliced

4 ripe pears, peeled, cored and thickly sliced

8 plums, halved and stoned (pitted)

1½ cups/225 g/8 oz blackberries

½ cup/100 g/4 oz sugar

1¼ cups/300 ml/½ pt water

Place the lemon rind in a saucepan. Put the juice
into a dish for coating the apples and pears. Pare a
strip of rind from one orange, then add it to the
lemon rind. Cut all the peel and pith from the
oranges, then cut out all the fruit segments from
between the membranes. Do this over the saucepan
to catch all the juices. Squeeze any remaining juice
from the membranes.

Dip the apples and pears in lemon juice, place them
in a bowl with the orange segments. Lightly mix in
the plums and sprinkle in the blackberries.

Add the sugar and water to the fruit peel. Bring to
the boil stirring, then boil for 5 minutes to reduce the
syrup. Cool slightly, then strain the syrup over the
fruit. Leave until cold before serving.

# 9

# CAKES, PASTRIES AND BISCUITS

Polish baking reflects the best from the surrounding countries as well as the influence of many foreign rulers. The recipes in this chapter merely hint at the variety and versatility of the mouthwatering delights of Polish home baking or the specialities of cafés and coffee houses. Taking afternoon coffee and cake is a social event, an opportunity to meet friends or to entertain guests. Inviting friends for coffee and cake is a more common event than a dinner party, whether the refreshment is organised at home or at a pâtisserie.

As in other countries, traditional cakes are a feature of seasonal festivities. For Christmas there is a poppy seed roll, little knotted biscuits or spiced cookies to hang on the Christmas tree; to celebrate Easter there must be a baba and cheesecake with, perhaps, a rich shortcake. The Saint's day whose name you share is the time for personal festivities, with a splendid high gâteau as the essential treat to be shared with family and friends.

As well as the socializing, the daily meals allow room for cakes and coffee as a regular filler, early in the afternoon or for a light snack later in the evening. In the south, Małgosia's home, the main meal is taken in the middle of the day rather than during the evening. Some form of sweet snack may well be served later in the day before, or instead of, a light supper.

Although some of the recipes in this chapter require extra effort and time for their preparation, they are well worth the work involved.

POLISH BABA

## POLISH BABA

Made for Easter the traditional decoration for baba is a small lamb moulded from sugar paste placed in the middle of the baba, with tiny Easter eggs all round and sprigs of fresh green foliage added. Makes a 23 cm/9 in baba.

*3 tsp (active) dried yeast or 25 g/1 oz fresh yeast (1 cake compressed yeast)*

*½ cup/100 ml/4 fl oz warm milk*

*scant 1 cup/100 g/4 oz icing sugar (confectioners' sugar)*

*4 cups/500 g/1 lb strong plain flour (hard wheat flour)*

*⅔ cup/100 g/4 oz raisins*

*⅓ cup/50 g/2 oz chopped candied peel*

*1 cup/100 g/4 oz blanched almonds, chopped*

*2 eggs, beaten*

*4 egg yolks*

*½ cup/100 g/4 oz butter, melted*

*icing sugar (confectioners' sugar) to dust or boiled icing (boiled frosting) (see note)*

Sprinkle the dried yeast over the milk and 1 tsp of the icing sugar (confectioners' sugar). Cream the fresh yeast with the milk and 1 tsp of the sugar. Leave in a warm place until frothy. Sift the flour into a bowl and mix in the fruit and nuts with the remaining icing sugar. Make a well in the middle, add the eggs, yolks, melted butter and yeast liquid. Mix the dry ingredients into the liquid to make a very soft dough. Beat this with your hand until very elastic and smooth (see page 71 for notes on this method). Cover and leave to rise in a warm place until doubled in size – about 2 hours.

Thoroughly grease a 9½ cups/2.1 L/3¾ pt kugelhopf mould or 26 × 14 cm/10½ × 5½ in (top measurement) loaf tin. Knock back (punch down) the dough with your hand, then put it in the tin pressing it down well. Cover loosely with cling film (plastic wrap) and leave in a warm place until the dough has risen to the top of the tin. Meanwhile, set the oven at 180°C/350°F/gas 4.

Bake the baba for about 40 minutes, until risen and well browned. Leave in the tin for a few minutes, then turn out to cool on a wire rack. Dredge with icing sugar or coat the baba with icing (frosting) while still warm. Leave to cool before serving, cut at a slant into slices.

**NOTE** To make boiled icing (boiled frosting), heat 1 cup/225 g/8 oz sugar with ⅔ cup/150 ml/¼ pt water and a pinch of cream of tartar until the sugar has dissolved, stirring occasionally. Bring to the boil and boil to the soft ball stage, 115°C/240°F on a sugar (candy) thermometer. Remove from the heat immediately and place the pan in cold water. Add 2 tbsp boiling water and beat the icing until it crystallizes and turns white. If the mixture becomes too thick and sugary, dilute with boiling water, a few drops at a time. Flavouring, such as coffee (1 tbsp instant dissolved in 1 tbsp boiling water) may be added to taste. To use the icing, melt it in a bowl over a pan of hot water, stirring until smooth.

## BABKA

This is a sponge cake. Dried fruit and candied peel may be added if liked. Makes 8–10 slices.

¼ cup/50 g/2 oz butter

scant 1 cup/100 g/4 oz icing sugar (confectioners' sugar), sifted

1 tsp natural vanilla essence (flavoring)

3 eggs, separated

¼ cup/50 ml/2 fl oz milk

1½ cups/175 g/6 oz plain flour (all purpose flour)

1 tsp baking powder

icing sugar (confectioners' sugar) to dredge

Base-line and grease a 19 × 11 cm/7½ × 4½ in loaf tin. Set the oven at 180°C/350°F/gas 4. Beat the butter in a bowl until very soft, then gradually beat in the icing sugar (confectioners' sugar). Stir in the vanilla and egg yolks, one by one. Slowly add the milk, mixing in the occasional small spoonful of flour to prevent the mixture from curdling. Sift the remaining flour with the baking powder and stir it into the mixture.

Whisk the egg whites until stiff and use a metal spoon to fold them in, taking care not to knock out the air. Turn the mixture into the tin and spread it with the back of a metal spoon, hollowing out the middle slightly.

Bake for 40–45 minutes, until risen and golden. Turn out the babka to cool on a wire rack. Dredge with icing sugar while still warm.

## GYPSY CAKE

This cake is based on another tip from the helpful lady in the Polish delicatessen. Since the store is some distance from where I live I have not taken her a sample for confirmation that the result is authentic, but I followed her verbal recipe and this cake tastes good. It is good just as it is or I found it very tempting when sandwiched with plum spread. Makes about 10 pieces.

6 eggs, separated

½ cup/100 g/4 oz caster sugar (superfine sugar)

1 tsp natural vanilla essence (flavoring)

1 cup/100 g/4 oz plain flour (all purpose flour)

1 tsp baking powder

⅓ cup/50 g/2 oz raisins

⅓ cup/50 g/2 oz dried figs, chopped

⅓ cup/50 g/2 oz cooking dates, chopped if necessary

3 tbsp/25 g/1 oz chopped mixed peel

icing sugar (confectioners' sugar) to dredge

Line and grease a 28 × 18 cm/11 × 7 in tin (a shallow tin is fine, in which case the greaseproof (waxed) paper should stand well above the rim). Set the oven at 200°C/400°F/gas 6.

Cream the egg yolks and sugar in a bowl until pale and thick. Lightly stir in the vanilla, then fold in the flour and baking powder. Stir in all the fruit. Whisk the egg whites until stiff and stir a couple of spoonfuls into the mixture to lighten it, then fold in the remainder. This is not easy as the mixture is fairly stiff but try not to over-stir while mixing in the whites. Turn the mixture into the tin and spread it out.

Bake for about 20 minutes, or until risen, golden and firm to the touch. Cool on a wire rack. Dredge with icing sugar (confectioners' sugar) before serving cut into oblong pieces.

## POPPY SEED ROLL

Makowiec, as it is known, is made for Christmas eve. A rich and delicious yeast dough encircles a fruity poppy seed filling. It is essential that the poppy seeds are sweet, not at all bitter or musty. I made one using poppy seeds that were, I discovered later, bitter and the result was very disappointing. Makes 1 large cake (about 20 slices).

2 tsp (active) dried yeast or 20 g/¾ oz fresh yeast (¾ cake compressed yeast)

¼ cup/50 g/2 oz caster sugar (superfine sugar)

½ cup/100 ml/4 fl oz warm milk

3 cups/350 g/12 oz strong plain flour (hard wheat flour)

1 egg, beaten

6 tbsp/75 g/3 oz butter, melted

**FILLING**

1 cup/175 g/6 oz poppy seeds, ground (page 11)

¼ cup/50 g/2 oz butter

½ cup/100 g/4 oz sugar

½ cup/75 g/3 oz raisins

⅓ cup/50 g/2 oz candied orange peel, finely chopped

½ tsp ground cinnamon

boiled icing (boiled frosting) to decorate (page 85)

Sprinkle the dried yeast over the milk and 1 tsp of the sugar. Cream the fresh yeast with the milk and 1 tsp of the sugar. Leave in a warm place until frothy. Sift the flour into a bowl and mix in the remaining sugar. Make a well in the middle, add the egg and butter, then stir in the yeast liquid. Mix in the flour to make a soft dough. Knead the dough for about 15 minutes, until very smooth and elastic. Place in the bowl, cover with cling film (plastic wrap) and leave to rise in a warm place until doubled in size – about 2 hours.

Meanwhile prepare the filling: make sure the poppy seeds are well ground. Melt the butter in a small pan, add the ground seeds and cook, stirring, for a couple of minutes until the seeds are well combined and smell nutty. Stir in the remaining filling ingredients and set aside to cool.

Cut a double thick piece of firm, non-stick baking parchment measuring about 45 × 38 cm/18 × 15 in. This will be formed into a tube to keep the dough in shape as it rises, so the paper must be fairly stiff. Brown paper lined with greased greaseproof (waxed) paper may be used instead.

Knock back (punch down) the dough. Lightly flour the surface and roll out the dough to an oblong measuring 34 × 25 cm/13½ × 10 in. Spread the filling over the dough, leaving a 2.5 cm/1 in border around the edge. Roll up the dough from the long side. Pinch the dough together all along the join and pinch the ends of the dough to seal in the filling. Carefully lift the roll on to the paper and bring the paper up to form a cylinder around it. Overlap the edges of the paper and secure the roll with tape and or staples, or use pins. Leave to rise in a warm place until doubled in size – about 1 hour. Meanwhile, set the oven at 220°C/425°F/gas 7.

Bake the roll in its paper for 30 minutes, until firm and well browned. Open the paper roll, removing all pins etc carefully, and leave to cool. Coat with icing while the roll is still warm, then leave to cool completely.

**NOTE:** It is not essential to the success of the dough to put it in the tube of paper while proving and baking, but it is necessary to give the makowiec its proper shape. The first one I made flattened out slightly as it proved and more so as it was baking: a lady in a Polish delicatessen passed on this professional tip about using the roll of paper.

POPPY SEED ROLL

## PIERNIK

This is a honey cake, although it is often described as gingerbread because of its colour and the combined flavour of other spices and honey rather than the ingredients. It should be stored for at least a week before it is eaten, preferably a few weeks so that it has time to soften. The piernik will keep, and it is traditionally kept, for several months. The uncooked dough may be left for several days, even weeks, before it is baked. A piece of piernik is added to the sauce for Christmas eve carp (page 30) in old recipes for this dish. Makes a 20 cm/8 in square cake.

| |
|---|
| ¾ cup/225 g/8 oz clear honey |
| 1 tsp ground cinnamon |
| 4 cloves |
| ½ tsp grated nutmeg |
| 3 cups/350 g/12 oz plain flour (all purpose flour) |
| 2 tsp bicarbonate of soda (baking soda) |
| ¼ cup/50 g/2 oz butter |
| ¼ cup/50 g/2 oz sugar |
| ⅓ cup/50 g/2 oz candied orange peel, finely chopped |
| ⅓ cup/50 g/2 oz raisins |
| ⅓ cup/50 g/2 oz sultanas (white raisins) (optional) |
| about ½ cup/50 g/2 oz hazelnuts (filberts) |
| 1 egg, beaten |

Heat the honey and spices in a small pan until boiling. Reduce the heat so the honey is just boiling for 3–4 minutes, until darkened. Put the pan into cold water and stir 1 tsp cold water into the honey. Leave to cool. Remove the cloves. Base-line and grease a 20 cm/8 in square deep cake tin. Set the oven at 180°C/350°F/gas 4.

Sift the flour and bicarbonate of soda (baking soda) into a bowl. Rub in the butter, then stir in all the dry ingredients. Mix in the honey and egg. Turn the mixture on to a floured surface and knead well – the dough is soft but keep it moving to prevent it from sticking. Turn the dough into the tin, pressing down evenly. Bake for 50–60 minutes. The piernik is cooked when a skewer inserted into the middle comes out free of any sticky mixture. Cool the piernik on a wire rack, then wrap in cling film (plastic wrap) and a plastic bag to mature.

**NOTE:** Piernik is used in a number of ways. It may be used as the basic recipe for making biscuits

PIERNIK

(cookies), it may be sandwiched together with a jelly (such as redcurrant jelly) and topped with melted chocolate or it may be assembled in many layers and iced with chocolate or boiled icing (boiled frosting) (page 85) to make a Christmas cake. A filling of dried and bottled fruits with nuts and orange rind would be used for this. I bought piernik that was sandwiched in two layers with a thick filling of tangy fruit jelly, topped with a mixture of sweetened ground almonds and Polish spirit (it was similar to an excellent almond paste), then coated in chocolate – perfect tasting and not too sweet.

ICED MAZUREK

## ICED MAZUREK

Plain mazurek is a type of shortbread, which may be iced and cut into fingers to serve at Easter. I also include a chocolate mazurek, made with nuts and grated chocolate instead of the flour. This recipe makes 16 pieces.

| |
| --- |
| *2 cups / 225 g / 8 oz plain flour (all purpose flour)* |
| *2 tsp baking powder* |
| *½ cup / 100 g / 4 oz butter* |
| *⅔ cup / 75 g / 3 oz icing sugar (confectioners' sugar), sifted* |
| *2 egg yolks* |
| ***DECORATION*** |
| *boiled icing (boiled frosting) (page 85)* |
| *candied orange peel, cut into strips* |
| *about ¼ cup / 50 g / 2 oz glacé cherries (candied cherries), quartered* |
| *about 2 tbsp flaked almonds (slivered almonds), toasted* |

Sift the flour and baking powder into a bowl. Rub in the butter and mix in the icing sugar. Blend in the egg yolks to make a soft dough. Wrap in cling film (plastic wrap) and chill for 5 minutes. Meanwhile, base-line and grease a 20 cm/8 in square cake tin. Set the oven at 180°C/350°F/gas 4.

On a floured surface, roll out the dough into a square. Put it into the tin and press out with your fingers to cover the base of the tin. Make sure the top is smooth and the dough evenly thick.

Bake for about 35–40 minutes, until golden and firm. Turn out to cool on a wire rack. Coat with icing and decorate when cool. Cut into fingers to serve.

## MAZUREK

This improves with keeping for a couple of days before topping with chocolate and eating. Makes about 22 pieces.

*3 eggs, separated*

*½ cup/100 g/4 oz caster sugar (superfine sugar)*

*½ cup/50 g/2 oz plain flour (all purpose flour)*

*½ lb/225 g/8 oz plain chocolate (semi sweet chocolate), coarsely grated*

*1 cup/225 g/8 oz ground almonds*

### DECORATION

*1⅓ cup/225 g/8 oz redcurrant jelly*

*⅔ cup/100 g/4 oz plain chocolate (semi sweet chocolate), broken into pieces*

*¼ cup/50 g/2 oz unsalted butter*

Line and grease a 28 × 18 cm/11 × 7 in tin (a shallow tin is fine, in which case the greaseproof (waxed) paper should stand well above the rim). Set the oven at 200°C/400°F/gas 6.

Cream the egg yolks and sugar in a bowl until pale and thick. Lightly fold in the flour. Whisk the egg whites until stiff and fold them into the mixture. Lightly stir in the chocolate and almonds. Turn the mixture into the tin and spread it out evenly.

Bake for 20–25 minutes, until firm and lightly browned. Cool the mazurek in the tin for 5 minutes, then turn out on to a wire rack to cool completely.

For the decoration, warm the redcurrant jelly in a bowl over hot water and spread it all over the mazurek. Leave to set completely, then chill for 30 minutes. Melt the chocolate and butter in a bowl over hot water. Leave to cool but do not allow the mixture to thicken. Pour the chocolate all over the mazurek and spread it evenly. Leave to set before cutting into fingers.

## CHEESECAKE

This baked cheesecake, called sernik, has a firm texture and deep golden-coloured crust. Polish cottage cheese is far firmer than the soft curds sold in cartons, so it took several attempts to achieve a recipe that is similar to the authentic baked cheesecake. Sernik is made for Easter, whether it be this version, the double-crust cheesecake (see note), cheese placek (page 91) or a cheesecake baked on a sponge base. Serves about 10.

### BASE

*1½ cups/175 g/6 oz plain flour (all purpose flour)*

*1 tsp baking powder*

*½ cup/100 g/4 oz unsalted butter*

*4 tbsp caster sugar (superfine sugar)*

*2 egg yolks*

### TOPPING

*2 cups/500 g/1 lb curd cheese or quark*

*½ cup/100 g/4 oz sugar*

*¼ cup/25 g/1 oz plain flour (all purpose flour)*

*⅓ cup/50 g/2 oz candied orange peel, chopped*

*⅔ cup/100 g/4 oz raisins*

*grated rind of 1 lemon*

*4 eggs, separated*

*icing sugar (confectioners' sugar) to dredge*

For the base, sift the flour and baking powder in a bowl. Rub in the butter, then stir in the sugar. Mix in the yolks to make a soft dough. Grease a 25 cm/10 in springform tin or loose-based cake tin and press the dough into it. Chill for 15 minutes. Set the oven at 190°C/375°F/gas 5. Bake the base for 10 minutes, then set aside to cool. Reduce the oven temperature to 170°C/325°F/gas 3.

For the topping, place the cheese in a double thick piece of scalded muslin (cheesecloth) and squeeze as much liquid as possible from it (avoid squeezing the cheese through the cloth). Scrape all the cheese into a bowl, then beat in the sugar, flour, fruit, lemon rind and egg yolks. Whisk the whites until stiff, fold them into the mixture. Turn the mixture on top of the prepared base. Spread the cheese mixture evenly.

Bake for 1¼–1½ hours, until well browned, risen and fairly firm to the touch. Leave the cheesecake to cool in the tin. Dredge with icing sugar (confectioners' sugar) before serving.

**NOTE:** To make a double-crust cheesecake, double the quantity of the base ingredients and save half until the cheesecake topping is in place. Roll out the reserved dough and trim it to fit the top of the tin. Lift it carefully on top of the cheesecake and bake as above.

## COFFEE GÂTEAU

This light gâteau is just a sample of the type of layered cakes that are made for all celebrations. As well as the traditional Christmas dishes, in some households at least two gâteaux would be prepared. Makes a 25 cm/10 in gâteau.

8 eggs, separated

²/₃ cup/150 g/5 oz caster sugar (superfine sugar)

1½ cups/175 g/6 oz plain flour (all purpose flour)

**FILLING AND COATING**

2 tbsp cornflour (cornstarch)

2 tbsp sugar

1 cup/250 ml/8 fl oz milk

6 egg yolks

1 cup/225 g/8 oz unsalted butter

scant 1½ cups/175 g/6 oz icing sugar (confectioners' sugar), sifted

1 tbsp instant coffee

2 tbsp boiling water

boiled icing (boiled frosting) flavoured with coffee (page 85)

1 cup/100 g/4 oz walnuts, chopped

Line and grease a 25 cm/10 in deep, loose-based cake tin, with the paper standing about 5 cm/2 in above the rim of the tin. Set the oven at 180°C/350°F/gas 4.

Cream the egg yolks and sugar in a bowl until very pale and thick. Use a large metal spoon to lightly fold in the flour. Whisk the egg whites until stiff and stir a spoonful of them into the mixture, then lightly fold in the remainder. Turn the mixture into the tin. Bake for about 45 minutes, until the cake is well risen, golden and springy to the touch. Turn out of the tin and cool on a wire rack.

For the filling, blend the cornflour (cornstarch) with the sugar and milk. Bring to the boil, stirring all the time. Off the heat, add the egg yolks, then return the pan to the heat and cook gently until thickened. Cover the surface of the custard with cling film (plastic wrap) or greaseproof (waxed) paper and leave until cold. Beat the butter until creamy, then gradually beat in the icing sugar (confectioners' sugar) until very soft. Stir in the custard, a spoonful at a time. Dissolve the coffee in the boiling water. Cool, then stir it into the cream.

Cut the cake into four layers and sandwich them together with some of the coffee cream. Spread coffee icing over the top of the cake. Leave this to set slightly before spreading a little cream around the side of the cake. Press the nuts on to the side. Put the remaining coffee cream in a piping bag (pastry bag) fitted with a star nozzle. Pipe swirls of cream all around the top edge of the gâteau.

COFFEE GÂTEAU

CHEESE PLACEK

# CHEESE PLACEK

This lattice-topped cheese tart is slightly more delicate than sernik. Serves 8.

### PASTRY

*2 cups/225 g/8 oz plain flour (all purpose flour)*

*3 tsp baking powder*

*6 tbsp/75 g/3 oz unsalted butter*

*¼ cup/50 g/2 oz caster sugar (superfine sugar)*

*1 egg*

*3 tbsp soured cream*

### FILLING

*2½ cups/600 g/1¼ lb cottage cheese*

*½ cup/100 g/4 oz sugar*

*2 tbsp plain flour (all purpose flour)*

*½ tsp natural vanilla essence (flavoring)*

*grated rind of 1 lemon*

*3 eggs, separated*

*icing sugar (confectioners' sugar) to dredge*

Grease a 28 × 20 cm/11 × 8 in loose-based oblong flan dish. For the pastry, sift the flour and baking powder into a bowl. Rub in the butter, then stir in the sugar. Mix in the egg and soured cream to make a soft dough. Set aside one-third of the dough, then use the rest to line the base and sides of the tin. Prick the base all over, then chill the dough for 30 minutes.

Set the oven at 190°C/375°F/gas 5. Line the dough case with greaseproof (waxed) paper and sprinkle with dried peas. Bake blind for 15 minutes. Remove the paper and cool.

For the filling, place the cheese in a double thick piece of muslin (cheesecloth) and squeeze as much liquid as possible from it. Press the drained cheese through a sieve, then beat in the sugar, flour, vanilla, lemon rind and egg yolks. Whisk the whites until stiff and fold them into the mixture. Turn the mixture into the prepared base.

Roll out the reserved dough into an oblong about the same size as the placek, then cut it lengthways into 1 cm/½ in wide strips. Arrange these in a lattice over the filling, trimming and re-rolling as necessary. Bake for about 35–40 minutes, until browned on top and firm. Leave to cool, then dust with a little icing sugar (confectioners' sugar). Cut into squares to serve.

## PLUM PLACEK

Instead of the base used here, a rich yeast dough may be rolled out and filled with plums. A crumble topping of half and half butter and flour rubbed together, sweetened with a little sugar, may be sprinkled over the plums if a yeast base is used. Serves 8.

| |
|---|
| 1½ cups/175 g/6 oz plain flour (all purpose flour) |
| 1 tsp baking powder |
| 3 tbsp caster sugar (superfine sugar) |
| ¼ cup/50 g/2 oz butter |
| 1 egg yolk |
| 3 tbsp soured cream |
| a little egg white |
| 1¼ lb/600 g/1¼ lb large plums, quartered and stoned (pitted) |
| icing sugar (confectioners' sugar) to dust |

Set the oven at 190°C/375°F/gas 5. Grease a loose-based oblong flan tin, measuring 28 × 20 cm/11 × 8 in. Sift the flour and baking powder into a bowl. Stir in the sugar and rub in the butter. Mix in the egg yolks and soured cream to make a soft dough.

On a lightly floured surface, roll out the dough to roughly the same size as the tin, then press it into the base of the tin. Brush with egg white. Arrange the plums on top of the dough, pressing them into the dough slightly.

Bake for 30–40 minutes, then cool slightly before dusting with icing sugar (confectioners' sugar). Serve hot, warm or cold.

## APPLE CAKE

Eva set me about making this 'cake' which she calls 'szarlotka'. It is good hot, warm or cold. Serves 8.

| |
|---|
| 3 cups/350 g/12 oz plain flour (all purpose flour) |
| ¾ cup/175 g/6 oz unsalted butter |
| ¼ cup/50 g/2 oz caster sugar (superfine sugar) |
| 2 egg yolks |
| 3 tbsp soured cream |
| ½ tsp vanilla essence (flavoring) |

***FILLING***

| |
|---|
| 1 lb/500 g/1lb cooking apples, peeled, cored and sliced |
| 4 tbsp sugar |
| 1 tsp ground cinnamon |
| icing sugar (confectioners' sugar) to dust |

Grease a 28 × 20 cm/11 × 8 in loose-based flan tin. Sift the flour into a bowl. Rub in the butter and stir in the sugar. Mix in the egg yolks with the soured cream and vanilla to make a soft dough. Divide into two portions, one slightly larger than the other. Roll out the larger portion and use to line the base and sides of the tin. Chill for 15 minutes.

Set the oven at 190°C/375°F/gas 5. Line the dough case with greaseproof (waxed) paper and sprinkle with dried peas. Bake blind for 15 minutes. Remove the paper and cool.

Fill the prepared case with the apples, sprinkle with sugar and cinnamon. Roll out the remaining dough to cover the top and press the edges together firmly to seal in the filling. Bake for 40–45 minutes, until browned on top. Dust with icing sugar (confectioners' sugar). Serve warm or cold, cut into squares.

ONE OF THE PICTURESQUE LAKES IN CENTRAL POLAND.

APPLE PASTRIES

## APPLE PASTRIES

These are slightly fiddly to make but they are worth the effort. Makes about 30.

| |
|---|
| *1½ cups/175 g/6 oz plain flour (all purpose flour)* |
| *6 tbsp/75 g/3 oz unsalted butter* |
| *3 tbsp caster sugar (superfine sugar)* |
| *½ cup/100 g/4 oz cottage cheese* |
| *2 tbsp soured cream* |
| *3 full-flavoured eating apples, peeled, cored and quartered* |
| *1 egg, beaten* |
| *icing sugar (confectioners' sugar) to dust* |

Sift the flour into a bowl. Rub in the butter and stir in the sugar. Drain any liquid from the cheese, then press it through a sieve. Mix the cheese and soured cream into the flour mixture to form a soft dough. Knead gently into a ball and cut in half.

Set the oven at 200°C/400°F/gas 6. Roll out one piece of dough quite thinly and cut out 6 cm/2½ in rounds, using a pastry cutter. Cut each apple quarter into two or three pieces. Place a piece of apple on a round of pastry. Brush the edge of the pastry with egg, then fold it in half to enclose the apple in a miniature pasty. Pinch the edges together to seal them well. Place the pasty on a greased baking sheet. Fill and seal all the pastry rounds, re-rolling the trimmings. Repeat with the second piece of pastry. Brush the pastries with beaten egg.

Bake for about 20 minutes, until golden and cooked. Cool on a wire rack and dust with icing sugar (confectioners' sugar) while warm. Serve warm or cold.

POPPY SEED PARCELS

## POPPY SEED PARCELS

These taste terrific! Makes 16.

*2 cups/225 g/8 oz plain flour (all purpose flour)*

*6 tbsp/75 g/3 oz unsalted butter*

*2 tbsp caster sugar (superfine sugar)*

*1 egg, separated*

*3 tbsp soured cream*

*½ cup/75 g/3 oz poppy seeds, ground (page 11)*

*2 tbsp/25 g/1 oz butter*

*4 tbsp raisins, chopped*

*2 tbsp clear honey*

*½ tsp grated nutmeg*

*caster sugar (superfine sugar) to sprinkle*

Sift the flour into a bowl. Rub in the butter, then stir in the sugar. Mix in the egg yolk with the soured cream to make a fairly stiff dough. Knead the dough, then wrap in cling film (plastic wrap). Chill for 30 minutes.

Meanwhile, make sure the poppy seeds are ground. Mix them with the butter in a small pan. Cook for a few minutes, stirring all the time. Add the raisins, honey and nutmeg and set aside to cool. Set the oven at 190°C/375°F/gas 5.

On a lightly floured surface, roll out the dough into a 35 cm/14 in square. Cut this into sixteen 8.5 cm/3½ in squares. Divide the poppy seed mixture between the squares, piling it in the middle of each with a teaspoon. Lightly whisk the egg white and brush it on the edges of the pastry. Fold the corners of each pastry square up to meet over the middle of the poppy filling. Pinch all the pastry edges together to seal them thoroughly. Use the blunt edge of a knife to knock the pastry edges down, holding them with two fingers, to ensure they are sealed and neat.

Place the parcels on greased baking sheets and brush them with a little egg white. Bake for 20–25 minutes, until golden. Sprinkle with caster sugar (superfine sugar) as soon as they are cooked. Cool on a wire rack.

## FAWORKI

The dough from which these biscuits (cookies) are made is called 'chrust'; sometimes the biscuits are also given this name. If you are inexperienced at making these little cookies, make sure you have enough time to get the knotting just right! They are sometimes made larger than here. Makes 24.

| |
| --- |
| *1 cup/100 g/4 oz plain flour (all purpose flour)* |
| *2 tbsp/25 g/1 oz butter* |
| *2 egg yolks* |
| *1 tbsp water* |
| *oil to deep fry* |

Sift the flour into a bowl and rub in the butter. Mix in the egg yolks and water to make a smooth dough. On a lightly floured surface, roll out the dough into an oblong measuring 45 × 15 cm/18 × 6 in and cut in half lengthways. Cut each half into twelve 3.5 cm/1½ in wide strips.

Take a strip of dough and cut a slit down the middle of it. Push one end of the dough through the slit, then flatten it out to make a neat little knot. Keep the dough covered with cling film (plastic wrap) while you knot and cook the strips, otherwise it dries out and breaks as you try to knot it.

Heat the oil for deep frying to 170°C/340°F. Fry the pastry knots in batches until crisp and golden. Drain them on double thick absorbent kitchen paper. Dust with icing sugar (confectioners' sugar) while hot. Cool on a wire rack.

FAWORKI

## CHRISTMAS TREE COOKIES

Use your imagination to ice and decorate these as elaborately as possible; better still involve the children and all the family when making them. Makes about 20.

| |
| --- |
| *3 tbsp clear honey* |
| *1 tsp ground cinnamon* |
| *pinch of ground cloves* |
| *½ tsp grated nutmeg* |
| *1 cup/100 g/4 oz plain flour (all purpose flour)* |
| *½ tsp bicarbonate of soda (baking soda)* |
| *2 tbsp/25 g/1 oz butter* |
| *1 egg yolk* |

### DECORATION

| |
| --- |
| *boiled icing (boiled frosting) (page 85)* |
| *crystallized and glacé fruits (candied fruits), angelica and any small sweets or cake decorations* |
| *thin red and green ribbon to hang the cookies* |

Bring the honey and spices to the boil. Boil for 2 minutes, then cool. Sift the flour and bicarbonate of soda (baking soda) into a bowl, then rub in the butter. Mix in the spiced honey and egg yolk to make a smooth dough. Chill for about 15 minutes.

Set the oven at 190°C/375°F/gas 5. Roll out the dough to 3 mm/⅛ in thick and cut out star-shaped cookies, measuring about 5.5–6 cm/2¼–2½ in across. Other shapes may be cut out using the variety of biscuit (cookie) cutters available. If you do not have shaped cutters, then cut round or diamond-shaped cookies. Place the cookies on greased baking sheets, slightly apart. Use a skewer to make a hole near the edge of each one. Bake for 8–10 minutes.

Cool on a wire rack. Make sure the holes are still open in the cookies before they cool.

Ice when cold. Press the decorations into the icing before it sets. Once the white icing has set, coloured icing may be used to write messages on the cookies. Pipe the icing through a greaseproof paper piping bag (waxed paper pastry bag) with the tip cut off (or use a fine nozzle in a bag, or cut the tiniest snip off the tip of a small, strong freezer bag).

Thread ribbon through the cookies when they are set and hang them on Christmas eve.

# INDEX